World's Funniest Cop Compilation

By

Dan Whitehurst

Table of Contents

Acknowledgement	1
Foreword	2
Massacre at Fort Nashborough	4
Three for Three	8
The Comment Card	13
Metro Police Comment Card	14
I've Got to Get Out of This Place	16
You're not supposed to laugh in a court of law	20
News of The Weird	24
Babysitting on the Clock	29
Lost A Bet	33
Who's Snitching?	36
He Made me Whoop Myself	43
Caught A Fat Girl	48
The Mayor of Shantytown	52
What are the Odds of that?	57
Big Jimmy Don't Like Snakes	63
The Fart Machine	68
Men and Dogs	71
They Never Just Quit on Their Own	76
You Might Know My Daughter	80
Sometimes I'm Not A Nice Person	83
With Apologies to Sergeant Stromatt	88
With Apologies to my Mother	94

Acknowledgments

I would like to thank the following people for the encouragement, motivation, memories and support without which I would have never sat down and finished this.

Mom and Dad for telling me I could, Janie and Tim Frizzell for letting me live with them during the eternity that was the Police Academy. Janet Williams who stayed on me more than Dad to finish this book. Leslie Nash for her technical assistance and patience when I wanted to shoot my computer. Brad and Yuki Beech for the friendship and life lessons. My uncle Frank Maples and my cousins, Officers David, Kevin and Timothy Moore and Aunt Alice. Drew Davis who helps more than he knows. The men and women of the Nashville Police Department and especially Sgt. Freddie Stromatt, Officer's Duane Williamson, Kenny Dyer, Norris Tarkington, Ron Riddle, Jeff Nidiffer, Cliff Craighead, Jerry Page and the best friend I ever had, J.R. Malone.

Foreword

I once won the title, "World's Funniest Cop". I also didn't win it a few of the times I competed, but you've got to admit that it's a pretty catchy title. I was Metropolitan Nashville Police Officer for a little over eighteen years. I like to say nineteen years and two months, but that includes the sick time and vacation days I rode out at the end of my career. I didn't consider police work a calling like most of the officers I worked with. I was simply trying to avoid doing manual labor. My attempt at getting a college degree didn't quite pan out. I was not really a fan of police officers in general, all I knew was that they didn't work in a factory.

At some point during my training at the Metropolitan Nashville Police Academy I experienced an attitude change. Maybe it was memorizing the names and situations which took the lives of the fallen Metro Police Officers over the years. Maybe it was realizing just how much a person had to give up just to become one. I believed that if I somehow made it through the academy, I would be the best police officer I could be, but deep down I had my doubts about whether or not that would be good enough for them. I have a bit of an immature streak.

For the record, I never had one suspension during my entire career. I probably should have been for a couple of things, but they didn't know it was me at the time. Like I said, I have a bit of an immature streak. I never once took a promotional exam because I didn't want to risk getting promoted. It was all I could do to keep myself in line. It's one thing to talk your coworkers into wearing Burger King crowns while conducting a search warrant, it's another to order subordinates to do so. I'm only guilty of the former.

When I look back at my career with the Metropolitan Nashville Police Department I know I wasn't the best and was certainly not the most professional police officer, but I know there are people whose lives were extended because I existed. I know I got to work with people who would risk their lives for strangers who didn't like them, and people who would run towards what was causing others to flee just because they repeated an oath swearing that they would. That was the biggest honor and I thank each one of the officers who served or are serving honorably across this nation.

I also thank every officer who ever made me laugh when I really needed it. I started writing these stories hoping to just share the funny ones. In order to paint a more complete picture of police work, at least my version of it, I added some that are not so funny.

Thank you for your interest.

Dan Whitehurst

Massacre at Fort Nashborough

The beauty of working downtown Nashville in the wintertime back in the mid nineteen-eighties was the mini vacation you got every morning from around 4 until 6 AM. The calls slowed down to the point you could go as long as forty five minutes without a dispatcher giving you an assignment. Except for the homeless, the downtown area became a virtual ghost town. There was an old saying about the only people moving around town at this time of day were the cops, the criminals and the dudes who make the donuts. Another, saying was that that idle hands were the devil's workshop.

I was in my second year with the Patrol Division and although I was normally assigned to the North Nashville Housing Projects, I also worked the down town zones when the schedule fell that way. It was a nice break from the hustle and bustle of Section Eight housing as few people actually lived downtown during that time.

One of my favorite time killers was driving to the top of one of the downtown parking garages and looking out over the city, microphone in hand, cord stretched to it's limit and the siren selector switch set on PA. From my vantage point I could occasionally spot someone looking in car windows or trying to use a wire to fish money out of the self-parking lot cash boxes. They could hear me talking to them, but had no idea where the booming voice came or who it was. I may not have actually stopped any crime, but I definitely moved it to another location.

It was from my perch atop a parking garage where I first heard the repeated hard acceleration of a vehicle followed by the sound of locking brakes. It peaked my curiosity to the point that I set out to see what exactly was going on. It was at First Avenue and Broadway where I initially spotted the source of the disturbance. From a distance I could see a marked Patrol Unit facing south on 1st Avenue in front of Fort

Nashborough, accelerating, backing up then accelerating again. I pulled my unit up on the sidewalk next to the old fort and got out to see what manner of mischief these officers had found to get into, I was not disappointed.

City rats are a different breed than rural rats. They are bigger scarier and more aggressive than their country cousins. They also have a mob mentality, fight one and you're going to fight them all. They have long yellow teeth and are about the size of an opossum.

The officers had discovered that if you tie a piece of rawhide to a string, throw the rawhide in the rat's direction, then start pulling the string, you could lead the rats like the pied piper. While one officer would lead the rats onto First Avenue, the second officer would try to run over them with his patrol car. While highly ineffective, it still provided quality entertainment. I immediately joined this band of like minded officers and added my touch of creativity to the festivities.

Although we never actually killed any rats, we did agree to meet back the next day around the same time and give it another shot, this time with B.B. guns. I put my Red Ryder B.B. gun in my patrol car as soon as I got home. I couldn't wait. For good measure, I also picked up a rat trap from the Farmer's Market, not a mouse trap mind you, but a rat trap. This thing could break a wrist.

The following day, at around 0345 hours the three of us showed back up next to Fort Nashborough looking for trouble. We got it.

The rats squeezed out of a hole that appeared far too small at the base of the Old Spaghetti Factory. They came one after the other like an assembly line on full throttle. You could run them back into the hole if you rushed them, yelling like wild men, but they started filing back out as soon as you stepped off the sidewalk. If the hole became crowded with fleeing rats, the others stuck outside would turn and challenge you. That's why we needed the B.B. guns. Hitting a rat with a night stick gave me a queasy feeling I didn't care much for.

It didn't take long to realize a spring propelled projectile was no match for a city rat. They might wince, but otherwise didn't appear harmed in the slightest. We ran the rats back into the hole, then placed the set but not baited rat trap at the base of the hole. The first rat to walk across it triggered it and it caught him right at the base of his neck, holding him in place as several rats climbed over his twitching body then spilled out onto the sidewalk. I watched in amazement as the trapped rat put both front paws at the base of the trap and slowly pulled his head out before sitting erect and looking around. This was starting to get a little scary.

The battle ended prematurely as the dispatcher called us away to respond to an actual human shooting near the Greyhound Bus Station. We agreed to meet back the next day with .22 caliber weapons. It was time to step up our game.

A .22 caliber short is a smaller round that doesn't make as much noise as the larger rounds. With the tall buildings, we assumed we could get off a few shots before anyone could tell exactly where the shooting was coming from. We assumed correctly as nobody ever called in to report shots being fired.

The following day was a slaughter. We killed about 15 rats, give or take. The sidewalk looked like the scene of a mighty battle, blood and bodies littered the area where businessmen and women would soon trod. Unable to leave well enough alone, I thought I would draw a chalk outline around a couple of the fallen. That led to propping up and posing a couple more deceased creatures which led to writing out a couple of suicide notes and leaving them next to the bodies.

We all got a bit of a kick out of it and we did it maybe two or three more times over the course of the next week or so.

Like all good things, this also came to an end. During a roll call given by the shift commander, he mentioned a complaint from the manager of the Old Spaghetti factory. I immediately got that little nervous feeling in the pit of my stomach, that one you get right before getting called out publicly.

"Whoever is killing the rats on 1st avenue, the manager of the spaghetti factory appreciates the effort but his employees are

threatening to quit if they keep having to clean it up. It's making them sick. Whoever is doing it and writing those notes stop now."
Just like that, the war had ended.

In nearly 19 years with the Nashville Metro Police Department, I never had one negative letter or justified complaint placed in my personnel file. I did however have several verbal reprimands addressed to "Whoever is doing this" over those nineteen years. Not too shabby.

Three for Three

"It's been one year since we graduated from the academy, how many people have you seen die?"

A former academy classmate asked as we were gathered in the roll call room.

The question oddly enough didn't seem out of line.

"None"

I replied.

"Really?"

I couldn't tell if he doubted me or the fact that I had made it a year without the experience of watching a human pass.

I had seen traffic fatalities, murder victims and several age or illness related human remains but I had never actually watched a person draw their last breath. My ability to use my first responder training remained a theory.

Later that same night I was working the 2200 to 0700 shift in North Nashville in what was known as zone 37 West. The zone included a set of apartments affectionately referred to as "Dodge City". From my understanding, the nick name for the complex started out as "Dark City" after a power outage, then due to miscommunication or the high number of shootings morphed into the current name. To this day I can't tell you what the official name of these housing projects were.

At the time, these particular apartments were one hundred percent black. While I couldn't identify each resident, I could easily spot some of the non-residents who came in, often to buy drugs.

During this particular shift I noticed a male and female white turning into the entrance to these projects in a dark colored vehicle as I drove past. A few moments later I drove back by and saw the vehicle coming out of the projects, driving slowly and using their blinkers at each turn. I followed the vehicle looking for any sort of infraction to give me cause to stop them. They never provided it. Each stop sign was met with a complete stop and every turn was accompanied by a turn signal. They obviously knew I was watching.

From my position behind the vehicle I could see only one person inside. I assumed the driver had dropped off his passenger thus giving him a legitimate reason to have been there in the first place. What bothered me though was the ultra cautious way he was driving. I turned off on a side street and let him continue on his way unobserved. I then pulled back out onto the street with my lights off and slowly retraced his route. Ultimately I came up on the vehicle stopped at an intersection. The driver had exited the vehicle and it appeared vacant. When he saw me approaching he walked to the front of the car and raised the hood. Thinking he was having car trouble I turned on my blue lights and got out of my car.

"Having trouble?" I asked.

"Yes, it does this at times," he replied with no noticeable distress in his voice.

As I walked past the driver's door of the subject 's vehicle I scanned the interior of the vehicle with my flashlight. The seat was vacant, but I could see what looked like a pile of blankets or something in the floor. I could not make out what it was.

"What's all that in your floorboard?" I asked more curious then concerned. "That's my wife, she's been shot." He replied with no emotion other than resignation in his voice.

I immediately call for an ambulance and as gently as I could pulled her from the floorboard of the vehicle where she had possibly slid after losing consciousness. I'm just guessing he had thrown the blanket over her.

The victim was thinly built, had dark hair and a small hole in the middle of her chest. She wasn't bleeding from the wound which I took to be a bad sign. She still had a pulse and erratic breathing when the ambulance arrived. I was holding her head in my lap as they approached and I felt her let go. That's the only word that comes to mind. She just let go.

The Metro Fire and Rescue personnel don't take defeat lightly. They valiantly tried to revive her both on the pavement and once they moved her into the ambulance. I could see them through the window trying to restart her heart with a defibrillator.
At this point I had no idea if the husband was the shooter or a grieving widower.

"What happened?" I asked.

"We were trying to buy drugs and a guy tried to rob us. He shot her as we tried to back out."

I got a quick description and put it out with the dispatchers and requested a Homicide unit meet with me. I later learned the husband was afraid of violating his probation and that was why he didn't want police assistance. I have no idea what his plan was, but it didn't appear to be helping his wife.

That is the story of the first time I saw a person die, on my one year anniversary. I wouldn't watch another person die until the following day.

One year and one day after graduation and I'm back in roll call. Tonight I will be working downtown. The most popular offense in the down town area is public drunk. The biggest offender was generally homeless people.

I enjoyed working downtown back in the day. Once the bars closed around 3 am, it became relatively quiet. Lower Broadway, the area of Broadway from 1st to 5th had some notoriously dangerous bars and adult businesses. The bars are now trendy, hip tourist attractions but in the day they were known more as dives by the locals.

At around 0230 hours, I rolled up Broadway from 1st avenue headed towards 5th. Right as I reached 5th I heard what sounded like a single shot. I made a u-turn and observed a male white stagger out of one of the bars and collapse in slow motion on the sidewalk. As I approached him I could see a small round hole in his shirt dead center of his chest. I put out a call to dispatch for an ambulance and checked on the victim who's breathing was erratic. I was telling the man that help was on the way but he never seemed to notice my presence. The ambulance was there very quickly and was getting out of the vehicle while I was holding my fingers on neck feeling his pulse getting weaker. "There he goes" I said as I felt the pulse end. The medics immediately began trying to revive the man using all the techniques that had been used on the woman the preceding night.

Apparently the man had been shot by the bartender. Detectives came to the scene and interviewed the shooter who claimed the shooting victim had been causing trouble and was asked to leave before attempting to attack the bartender who shot him from the other side of the bar. It was a fairly wide bar. I left never really knowing if it was self-defense or murder. The detectives would sort all that out.

After filling out a supplemental form detailing what I had heard and observed, I checked back into service with the dispatcher and was immediately given some sort of disturbance several blocks away.

Sometimes you really don't get a chance to reflect on one call before you're in the middle of another. The time for reflection can wait till you get home, climb in the bed and begin staring at the ceiling.

One year and two days after I graduated from the academy I responded to a report of a pedestrian struck by a car. I wasn't the first car on the scene, but I beat the ambulance.

The first officer on the scene was cradling a young boy, maybe 10 to 12 years of age. I could see him talking to the boy before his face contracted into an image I can still see to this day. Tears began flowing down his face as he hugged the now lifeless before turning it over to the arriving paramedics.

Dan Whitehurst

Just like that I had went from never watching a human die to seeing three pass in three days. That's about all I have to say about that.

The Comment Card

In-service training week was my least favorite week of the year. It wasn't anything the instructors did, I've never really enjoyed sitting in a classroom. My mind tends to wander off. I also had a nicotine habit and the academy had a no smoking/no dipping policy for the building. It always made me worry that I was going to get caught.

They also made us weigh in. Everyone in the Fat Boy Club would get a verbal or written reprimand, depending on how many times you have made the list. I think it took about three years of being on the list before the department would take a vacation day away.

The break room at headquarters had a few soda and snack machines that served as a cafeteria on those days when you worked around the clock. The machines usually had posted notes stuck to the front from detectives who were owed change or ripped off due to a malfunction. I once put a note on the snack machine claiming it owed me one vacation day. I put another detectives name on it.

There were some important classes taught at in-service training. Officer safety classes kept everyone updated on the new tactics found to be effective as well as keeping everyone aware of the ever- changing laws and policies. During those classes I tried to focus as best I could until I figured I had the gist of it.

I bailed much earlier if the class was taught by a non-sworn instructor and involved opinions that I didn't find valid. During one particular class I felt I didn't need, I created a comment card to secure the opinions of those non-sworn individuals who are very familiar with what being a law enforcement officer entails, the arrestees.
As best I remember, it went something like this;

Dan Whitehurst

METRO POLICE COMMENT CARD

Date/location of arrest _____

Please briefly state what the officer is trying to claim you did.
_____

Police Vehicle: Was it (A) Clean
                      (B) Dirty

Police Officer Name _____

Appearance. Did his or her appearance provide (A) Comfort
                                              (B) Discomfort

Use of Force. If force was used against you, do you feel the force was
(A) Justified
(B) Unjustified
(C) Hard to say, but Probably (B)

Booking Area/holding cell

Was it (A) Clean
       (B) Dirty

Cell Mate
(A) Friendly
(B) Unfriendly
(C) Too friendly

Would you recommend getting arrested in Metropolitan Nashville to your friends?

(A) With reservations
(B) With no reservations

    We do appreciate your business. We understand you could have gone anywhere and did that, but we appreciate you doing that here.

    Years later I saw a photostatic copy of this taped to the wall in the booking room. It made me giggle.

Dan Whitehurst

I've Got to Get Out of This Place

My first year of Patrol was awesome. Every shift was new and exciting. I hated my weekends and would sit and listen to the police radio for hours on my days off, keeping up with all the calls my friends were responding to. I wanted to be there. Evil was afoot and I needed to be out there with my people, plus I didn't really have much of a social life.

The second year it started to become a grind. Sure, every call was still different, but they were also all the same. Someone was hurt, someone was dead, someone was in fear or had been violated in any number of ways, somebody couldn't find their car keys. The one thing that never changed was that it was always something bad. That's the only reason they call.

I went from loving Patrol, to dreading the thought of doing thirty years of it soon after I completed my first full year. The exciting part of police work was losing its luster. I was burned out in just over one year.

I started constantly looking for diversions from the constant grind and daily routine. The midnight shift usually slowed down around four in the morning leaving enough officers in service that some of us got to grab a quick bite to eat and even back each other up on calls. I didn't always utilize the extra time wisely.

For instance, we had a flood downtown Nashville sometime in 1988 I believe. It was nothing like the flood of 2012, but it did cover the docking platform at Riverfront Park to a depth of about 3.5 feet. My friend and co-worker, Officer Jerry Page and I stood on the steps and watched the swirling water. It was about 0430 hours, or 4:30 AM if you prefer.

"You couldn't walk on that dock without getting swept away." Jerry said, making an observation I immediately disagreed with.

"Sure I could."

"I bet ten bucks that you can't" Jerry countered.

"Done". I pulled off my utility belt, with it's gun, radio, extra ammo and handcuffs and locked it in my patrol car.

"You're not really going to do it are you Chicken man?"

Chicken man was a name Jerry started calling me due to a recent habit I had developed of driving to the top of vacant parking garages and crowing like a rooster over the car's P.A. system each morning as the sun came up. Again, I did some weird things just to entertain myself.

I never answered, I just waddled down into the waist deep water. The current was pretty strong, but I stayed close enough to the railing to grab it if I felt in danger of getting swept away. As I turned to make my way back up to the steps, I heard Jerry call our sergeant, Louise Kelton and ask her to meet him at our location. She was already on lower Broadway, so she made it over before I ever got to my car to retrieve my gun belt.

"What are you doing?" She asked as I stood there with water flowing from my pants and boots and forming a puddle at my feet.

"I walked out on the dock. " I replied trying to sound like it wasn't such an unusual thing for a man to do.

"For what reason?" She asked ass if I might possibly have one.

"Money. I got paid ten dollars. I do this professionally."
"Go home and change your pants." She replied, with maybe a hint of resignation in her voice.

This wasn't the first time she caught me doing something a little left of center. She had been my immediate supervisor for over a year.

The first time I made her think I was a weirdo was on a robbery call on Jefferson street at a biker bar.

The bar had been robbed and I was on the scene taking a report. K-9 had also showed up as well as one of the local media reporters and her camera man.

Sgt. Kelton approached me and asked if I would mind giving a statement to the reporter.

"On TV?" I asked trying to appear more hesitant than I actually was.

"Sure on TV, what's the problem?"

"It's just that… It's just that my parents think I moved here to sell insurance." I answered without cracking a smile.

Sgt. Kelton took my report, spoke to the media and never mentioned it to me again. I later learned she told other supervisors that my parents thought I sold insurance and they told her that I was probably just messing with her.

Another case that comes to mind is a call myself and an officer named Jeff Wells answered at an adult business on Lower Broadway. A disorderly suspect had been threatening employees according to the call.

Upon our arrival, the suspect had already fled. We figured while we in there we would have a little look around. One thing led to another and before long we were sword fighting with two very long double ended phallic devices.

"Put the penises back and get back out there on the streets" Sgt. Kelton said, with authority.

We never saw her come in. She was pretty good.

One night while I was turning my paperwork into her she asked me if everything was ok. I could tell she was actually concerned as a friend and not just a supervisor, and I appreciated it.

"I'm just like everybody else, burnt out" I admitted.
She asked me where I would like to work outside of Patrol and I told her I would really like to work in the CSU unit one day as an undercover officer. Within a week I was assigned to the CSU unit working for one of the best Detective Sergeants I ever met. Freddie Dewayne Stromatt, the son of Lieutenant Stromatt. He was born to be a cop.

Unfortunately the CSU unit hadn't approved of my assignment to their unit and had someone else in mind. I probably didn't deserve the spot, but I got it nevertheless. The next four years were just like that first year in patrol. I absolutely had a ball. I grew my hair and beard till both went dropped below my shoulders. I drew jail house tattoos on my fingers. I traded my Yamaha for a Harley and I bought my first house next door to a lady who didn't know I was a cop. She hated me. The work in CSU was dangerous. Really dangerous. They had a car shot up in the "Dodge City" Projects just a few weeks prior to my assignment, narrowly missing the officers inside.

The majority of the time in CSU we dealt with street level drug or prostitution cases. Mostly drugs and mostly buying them from street dealers themselves. After making the buy we would grab hold of them and try to hang on till the back-up got there. I'm assuming it's similar to what a rodeo cowboy does. You just have to hang on for a few seconds. The cavalry is coming and they are coming hard and fast.
The guys in the unit also excelled at pushing the envelope when it came to practical jokes. It was like joining the circus.

YOU'RE NOT SUPPOSED TO LAUGH IN A COURT OF LAW

Court is serious business. The courtroom itself reeks of despair and nervous perspiration and becomes as solemn as a funeral home the moment the bailiff bellows, "ALL RISE!"

Laughter is generally considered as inappropriate in court as it would be at a wake. The more inappropriate it would be to laugh for the majority of us, the harder it is not to laugh. It works the same way in church.

My brother in law is a minister. He and my sister were attending a rural church in West Tennessee, three rows back from the front row, waiting for the service to begin. Seated in front of them was a man and his wife, seated in front of this couple were two women, one of which had a husband named Harold who was in the hospital.

The two women were discussing Harold, who was also a livestock farmer, and one of the women mentioned that he was nervous about those enemas. The husband seated behind the ladies thought she said "Animals" and leaned forward saying, "Yeah, he tried to give one to me last week". The two older women just looked shocked. My sister claimed she vibrated trying not to laugh out loud for the rest of the service.

I once lost it a little bit in court when a suspect used the following as a defense for domestic violence, "Your Honor, she knew there wasn't any liquor in the house when she paid the d*** light bill".

Court could often be the theatre of the absurd. I once saw a man charged with the armed robbery of a cab driver claiming innocence during the probable cause hearing. After his case was bound over to the grand jury, his attorney asked that the judge reduce the suspects bond.

The judge responded with the same speech he always gives when setting bond for a suspect. He had said it so many times he was actually reading something unrelated in a paper in his hand while he recited, "The purpose of bond is not to punish the defendant, but to assure the defendant will show up for subsequent hearings. Certain, more heinous crimes, such as armed robbery, rape, kidnappi…"

The suspect bolted from his chair, screaming,

"Rape! Rape! I didn't rape nobody! Sure, I robbed the man, but ya'll ain't gonna put no rape charge on me."

His attorney was trying to pull him back onto his seat the whole time he was yelling. The judge didn't even seem to crack a smile and of course the detective working the case was furiously writing down the admission noting the date, time and location.

It's tough to make a Judge laugh in court, but I did it once.

The case involved a suspect, who was known to me and who I had actually engaged in friendly conversation with multiple times. We knew each other by name and he hung out at the same market in my zone where I would eat lunch or take a break.

The call was about a burglary in progress at a home that had been vacated. The front door was standing open. I went in and saw the suspect sitting at a table cutting up an ounce or so of cocaine. We locked eyes, I said his name and then he bolted out the rear door. I chased him, yelling his name and telling him there would be warrants waiting on him as he slowly started to out distance me. I went back, bagged up the evidence and turned it into the property room then obtained warrants for possession for resale and unlawful flight.
I never saw the suspect again until about six months later. He had done a pretty good job of hiding. His attorney was someone who I

loved talking to and cutting up with, but he had a reputation of being a little on the shady side. (Years later he did a little time in prison).

During the probable cause hearing, the attorney went through the usual question as to how I was so sure it was him. I replied that I knew the suspect as well as I knew him. He repeated some vague questions wanting me to describe facial features of the suspect without looking at him, which I did and I must have been doing a pretty good job as he bailed on that line of questioning. Shady or not he was a very effective attorney and many officers hated to face him. He was good at implying officers planted evidence without actually saying it, and I thought that was the route he was about to take. Instead, he went back to the identification.

"Detective Whitehurst, may I remind you that you swore an oath to God to tell the truth in this court room today. With that in mind, can you swear you are 100% sure that my client is the one who ran from you?"

We had been over this so many times I decided to throw him a curve. I lowered my gaze as if in defeat.

"No".

His eyebrows arched and he seemed to catch his second wind. You could almost see the uncertainty in his eyes as he was debating accepting the "No" and being grateful for it, or rolling the dice and following it up.

He rolled the dice.

"How certain are you Detective?" His tone was softer, like he was rewarding me for my cooperation.

"Ninety Nine percent!" I said with no hesitation.

"But you're not one hundred percent sure?" He said as he desperately tried to correct the mistake he made by his gamble.

"Counselor," I responded.

"I'm not one hundred percent sure that any of this is actually happening."

The attorney flinched to the point both eyes blinked at the same time.

The judge? He laughed out loud.

Dan Whitehurst

News of The Weird

I was once mentioned in a News of The Weird article. I know it doesn't take much of a stretch of the imagination to see that happening. If you're not familiar with the segment, it's basically several very unusual news stories contained in a two-page spread in the local free papers. In Nashville the section was carried in the Nashville Scene. It was a couple of years after the incident before it made it into print. It wasn't the first time I saw something I was involved in resurface years later.

The first time was when I created a bogus comment card while sitting through an in-service class. I had handed it to an officer sitting next to me for his opinion and he handed it to the next guy and just like a bunch of school kids passing a note in class it made it's way around the room and disappeared.

As best I remember, it went something like this;

METRO POLICE COMMENT CARD

Date/location of arrest _____

Please briefly state what the officer is trying to claim you did.

_____

Police Vehicle: Was it (A) Clean
                          (B) Dirty

Police Officer Name _____

Appearance. Did his or her appearance provide (A) Comfort
                                                       (B) Discomfort

Use of Force. If force was used against you, do you feel the force was

(D) Justified
(E) Unjustified
(F) Hard to say, but Probably (B)

Booking Area/holding cell

Was it (A) Clean
         (B) Dirty

Cell Mate
(D) Friendly
(E) Unfriendly
(F) Too friendly

Would you recommend getting arrested in Metropolitan Nashville to your friends?
(C) With reservations
(D) With no reservations

    We do appreciate your business. We understand you could have gone anywhere and did that, but we appreciate you doing that here.

    Years later I saw a photostatic copy of this taped to the wall in the booking room. It made me giggle.

    During the times we did the buy/bust operations we often had to use force to effect the arrest. By often, I mean almost every time. I understand why a person would not immediately submit to being arrested by a man who just bought crack from him, but if we had to fight them, we had to fill out a use of force form. If a use of force form was filled out but the suspect was not charged with resisting, the officer could be hung out to dry, legally speaking. The charge was usually dropped as part of a plea deal.
    We started having a bit of a problem when one of the night court commissioners started denying resisting warrants on the grounds that she did not want us "Loading the suspects up with warrants".

As I stated earlier, almost every dealer resist arrest once the deal goes down. It's almost impossible for the buy officer to make an arrest on a street buy without several back up units coming in to seal off the escape routes. Freedom is the greatest motivator in the work for being fleet of foot.

We did pull it off once. Three of us were riding in a big four door Cadillac down 5th Avenue South after getting gas at the old Public Works building in the area. A subject attempted to flag us down in an area known for dilaudid sales as we drove by discussing whether or not we could catch him without any back up. For the record, I said we could not.

Sgt. Trickie made a u-turn and we headed back for another drive by. CSU Officer Chitty was in the front seat riding shotgun and I was in the back seat, probably eating something. The suspected dealer flagged us down, then ran up to the passenger side open windows and asked Sam what he wanted. Sam replied that he wanted one K-4, which is how the pills were marked and often referred to.

At this point I had my hand on the rear door handle, getting ready to bail out once the dealer grabbed the money. As Officer Chitty handed him the money with one hand, he tried to grab him with the other. The suspect broke free and took off like an Olympic Sprinter leaving Sam with both the Dilaudid Tablet and the sixty dollar asking price.

At the exact time I was about to advise everyone that I had won the bet, Sam Chitty pulled an ace from his sleeve. He told Sgt. Tricky to pull off slowly and he began laughing out the window loudly. The suspect stopped on a dime, turned and glared in our direction. You could almost see the wheels in his head turning as he was trying to decide if we were cops or guys who had just ripped him off. He decided it was the latter and ran at full speed towards the passenger side and dove headfirst through the open passenger side window. Getting him corralled became a piece of cake. I'm not sure if he was madder at us or himself. Probably us.

The absolute nicest, most cooperative drug dealer I ever arrested was also the one that the News of the Weird reported on. I had just purchased some crack from a man in the same area the window jumper had sold to us. I had just given the code word over the wire as I was handing him the money. I could hear the back up vehicles on the way. I grabbed his arm and said,

"Police"

He replied meekly,

"You got me"

That was it. I could have hugged him. I also told him I that I would definitely be mentioning it to the District Attorney. I think there should be some sort of reward for cooperation even if it's just a little. The suspect was a model prisoner all the way up until we were standing in night court in front of a huge night court crowd. It was right about the time I started giving my probable cause that the suspect morphed into something other than the polite young man from a few seconds before. He dropped to the floor on his hands and knees and started crawling in circles as fast as he could while barking loudly. I had paperwork in both hands and was looking around to see if someone could help me out while yelling,

"Sit! Bad! Sit! Stay!"

The crowd roared and the suspect leapt to his feet, lunged at the commissioner's elevated desk and was able to grab an affidavit off her desk in his teeth.

The commissioner screamed for us to get him out of there as I was trying to recover the affidavit by repeating loudly the word,

"Loose!"

The suspect pulled away from us at one point and struggled all the way out of night court until he immediately calmed back down in the booking room. I'm not really sure if he was leaving an insanity defense on the table or just playing for the crowd. He never said why he did it and I never asked him.

When I went back in to get the warrants signed, she gave me a good scolding in front of the night court crowd. My only defense was to explain that he was super cooperative until he heard her voice.

She was obviously angry at the man because she was prepared to also sign resisting warrants on him. I told her that was unnecessary because we required a little more than just passively pulling away for us to charge them with resisting. I hope she got the subtle reference.

Babysitting on the Clock

I worked in an undercover street level unit referred to as C.S.U, (Crime Suppression Unit) for four years. It was the most fun I ever had as a police officer. I got to grow a beard and long hair and even sported fake jailhouse tattoos I would always draw on my hands and fingers. Instead of love and hate, like most knuckle tattoos say, I would use "cows" or "teat" or something that made no sense at all. My new neighbor, who didn't know I was a police officer thought I was insane. I also rode a gangster looking Harley which added to the outlaw image I'm sure.

On one occasion a uniformed police officer friend of mine stopped by to say hello in his patrol car. We were talking in the front yard when the neighbor pulled in from work. She was obviously very curious about me and the heavy set cop talking in the driveway. She kind of smiled as she was fumbling for her keys, acting like she couldn't find them, all the while attempting to eavesdrop.

My friend was about to leave, so I whispered to him that she didn't know I was a cop and I was going to freak her out. He nodded, smiling and started to walk toward his car.

"And keep your fat ass off my property or you're going to get a mud hole stomped in you!" I yelled at him as he quickened his pace, now almost at his driver's door.

"Yes sir Mister Whitehurst, it will not happen again," he replied as he jumped in his car and accelerated with enough force to break the tires loose on the pavement.

I glanced at the neighbor who was standing dumbfounded with her house keys in her hand. She quickly got the door open then slammed it behind her as she retreated to her safe space.

We seldom dealt with victims. Either we were arresting drug dealers who sold us crack in hand to hand undercover buys, or we did search warrants or wrote citations to prostitutes who propositioned us. We didn't deal with the heartache of working with victims of violent crime directly. We were constantly exposed to people whose own lives they had ruined, but we mostly worked what many refer to as victimless crimes.

That's not to say we never had our hearts broken working the so called victimless crimes.

The drug world can be a scary place. Rip offs are common. Most of the "Dealers" we dealt with were addicts themselves. They supported their habits by selling their drug of choice. As you can imagine, they usually burn all their bridges pretty quickly as far as getting drugs fronted to them. If they were not holding, they would asked for the money up front to go get the drugs. If you gave them money upfront they wouldn't come back. The trick was having them leave something with you that they wanted more than ripping you off. It could be their shoes, a jacket, pretty much anything they would come back for. If the shoes were worn out, then you just bought a pair of shoes, so you had to pay attention during negotiations.

One night Officer Duane Williamson and I were sitting in a beat up undercover vehicle in the housing projects near a known drug area. It wasn't a very well-lit area. A middle aged man approached us and asked what we needed. Standing a few feet away was a female about half his age holding an infant on her hip.

"We're looking for a twenty" I replied, which means a twenty dollar rock of cocaine.

"I'm going to need the money up front" He said, with a tone more hopeful than it should have been.

"That's not going to happen." Officer Williamson replied.

"What if I leave my shoes?" He asked while pulling off a well-worn flip flop and offering it for inspection.

Before either of us had a chance to respond, the female stepped up to the car and handed a one year old infant through the window to officer Williamson.

"Ya'll can hold this baby. We ain't going to rip you off."

I handed him twenty dollars and both of them walked off into the shadows.

Duane and I looked at each other. The baby looked at both of us, first one and then the other. He was wearing only a diaper. He appeared healthy, he wasn't crying or acting as if he was in any distress, but he was a little dirty.

The vehicle was wired so the backup units could hear what was going on.

"Well Sgt. you're not going to believe this one, they left us a baby," Duane said for the backups benefit.

"We're waiting for them to come back, but go ahead and notify Juvenile and the Department of human services."

You somewhat get used to man's inhumanity to man when you see it so very often, but I'm not sure I could ever get used to something like this. It was so heartbreaking and he was so brave. He was fascinated by my beard and never offered to cry once.

"You ain't got no kids Dan, why don't you just take him home" Duane joked.

"You've got five, how's one more going to hurt?" I replied.

We then joked around about renting him out in our rent a baby program, which we had come up with months before after noticing the percentage of defendants who show up to court with their babies in tow. We felt a little bad for the dads without babies on sentencing day, they don't get to play the Daddy card.

Eventually the mother came back to our vehicle demanding her baby.

"Not till we get our dope" Duane told her as I held the child.

"I don't know where he ran off to" She said.

"Then you ain't getting the baby."

We then placed her under arrest, turned the baby over to a DHS worker and obtained warrants for the male after learning his name.

I've often wondered whatever happened to that little boy. I like to think he became one of those rags to riches stories. He's 27 years old now.

If he survived.

Lost a bet

During the times we did the buy/bust operations during the Crime Suppression Unit days, we often had to use force to effect the arrest. By often, I mean almost every time. I understand why a person would not immediately submit to being arrested by a man who just bought crack from him, but if we had to fight them, we had to fill out a use of force form. If a use of force form was filled out but the suspect was not charged with resisting, the officer could be hung out to dry, legally speaking. The charge was usually dropped as part of a plea deal. We started having a bit of a problem when one of the night court commissioners started denying resisting warrants on the grounds that she did not want us "Loading the suspects up with warrants".

As I stated earlier, almost every dealer resist arrest once the deal goes down. It's almost impossible for the buy officer to make an arrest on a street buy without several back up units coming in to seal off the escape routes. Freedom is the greatest motivator in the work for being fleet of foot.

We did pull it off once. Three of us were riding in a big four door Cadillac down 5th Avenue South after getting gas at the old Public Works building in the area. A subject attempted to flag us down in an area known for dilaudid sales as were driving by, discussing whether or not we could catch him without any back up. For the record, I said we could not.

I never thought he would let us try, but Sgt. Trickie made a u-turn and we headed back for another drive through the area. CSU Officer Chitty was in the front seat riding shotgun and I was in the back seat, probably eating something. The suspected dealer flagged us down, then ran up to the passenger side open windows and asked Sam what he wanted. Sam replied that he wanted one K-4, which is how the pills were marked and often referred to.

At this point I had my hand on the rear door handle, getting ready to bail out once the dealer grabbed the money. As Officer Chitty handed him the money with one hand, he tried to grab him with the other. The suspect broke free and took off like an Olympic Sprinter leaving Sam holding both the Dilaudid Tablet and the sixty-dollar asking price.

At the exact time I was about to advise everyone that I had won the bet, Sam Chitty pulled an unexpected ace from his sleeve. He told Sgt. Tricky to pull off slowly and he began laughing out the window loudly. The suspect stopped on a dime, turned and glared in our direction, trying to decide if we were cops or guys who had just ripped him off. He decided it was the latter and ran at full speed towards the passenger side and dove headfirst through the open passenger side window. Sam grabbed him briefly before he broke free, backed off and then took one more running leap at us to see if he could make it all the way into the car. He made it all the way in on his second attempt with our help.

Once he realized that we were police officers for real and that we had a pretty good grip on him, he gave up and allowed himself to be handcuffed. I almost felt sorry for him, like those poor souls with outstanding warrants and show up to receive one of those bogus prizes the warrant office promised them.

He kept shaking his head and muttering to himself,

"Oh man, oh man, oh man, stupid, stupid, stupid"
The closest I ever came to seeing someone with that look before was from a man who sold me crack cocaine for the second time in the span of three months. When he initially flagged me down, he

said I looked like the cop that had busted him last time. He even remembered that I had a tattoo on my ankle. His face didn't ring a bell with me. It took some doing, but he eventually decided I just looked a whole lot like that cop.

He was actually a pretty nice guy for a crack dealer. He gave up without a fuss, only offering up the following concession,

"You got me, again"

Who's Snitching?

There is a line in the movie Scarface (The early 80's version) that seems appropriate for this chapter.

"Don't get high on your own supply".

Al Pacino disregards this advice near the end of the movie and is shot to death while being high on his own supply. The following is not nearly so dramatic.

I was in The Crime Suppression Unit, in an unmarked car in an area where residents had complained about the high number of street dealers. In some neighborhoods street dealers are like aggressive pan handlers. They flag cars down and even go as far as stepping out in front of moving cars to try and make a sale. Sometimes they rob those who stop, sometimes they make a sale.

I had not even made it all the way into the target area when I was flagged down by a male white, mid-twenties with short blond hair. "What you needing?" He said as he opened the unlocked passenger door and seated himself without an invitation.

I had tossed my portable radio under the seat a few seconds before he sat down, my timing was on point. I wasn't one hundred percent sure if I had turned it off though.

We were looking for a suspect selling out of particular house in the area. He was reputed to be selling lots of marijuana in the neighborhood. This was not him.

"Just a quarter of weed." I responded.

"Head down towards Nolensville road, I got a dude." He replied.

As I turned left onto Nolensville road, I could hear static coming from under the seat. I cranked the AM/FM radio up but could still hear a faint muffled voice from down under saying,

"He's turning left on Nolensville road."

The suspect cut his eyes at me,

"Did you hear something?"

"Yeah that was weird." I said and for whatever reason it seemed to placate him. We didn't deal with rocket scientists.

We pulled into a driveway on Vivelle Avenue with the stereo blasting. He wanted me to give him the money and let him get the weed from the dealer. I told him I would just go in with him instead.

The entire transaction took about a minute. A man in jeans and a t shirt handed me around a quarter ounce of weed and I handed him 40 bucks. My rider and I got back in the under cover vehicle and pulled away headed back in the direction of Nolensville road.

My rider didn't seem to have a worry in the world. Little did he know a marked unit was about to stop us, remove him from the vehicle, search him, question him, write him a State Citation and then let him go. Had he known in advance he might very well have still done the deal.

Marijuana was pretty low on the importance scale even way back then. We never targeted weed dealers on our own because there was never much of a result from all the work one had to invest. However, if someone goes out of their way to complain about pot dealers in a particular area we were obligated to act.

The stop went smoothly and the suspect was relatively cooperative. By relatively, I mean he did not actively fight.

He was given his citation and sent on his way from the area he was picked up in.

This is where it gets good.

     I was asked to go back and get the guy who sold me the quarter. I drive back to the house, got out of the car and noticed a young teenage girl standing on the porch.

"Are you here to see Daddy?" She asked.

"Yes I am".

     I walked through the door as she held it open and I heard it close as she wandered off the porch headed for where ever it was she was going. I held my badge cupped in my hand where it was hidden from view as I looked around the room. I spotted who I believed to be the suspect sleeping face down on the couch.

"Police."

I said, in an average speaking tone while tapping him lightly on the shoulder with my badge. This was going to be a piece of cake.

"What do you want?"

The man replied as he struggled to awake.

It was at this point that I realized this was not the same man.

I said the first thing that popped into my head.

"I need a quarter."

"Why didn't you say so!"

     He responded, now totally awake. He rose from the couch and walked down the hallway briskly.

"Just give me one minute."

I assumed he was going to bring me one quarter, I would arrest him, ask for consent to search, be refused and spend the rest of the evening typing up a search warrant. I was wrong.

"Pick you one out!"

The suspect exclaimed as he poured around 20 quarter ounce bags of marijuana from a paper shopping bag. I stood there looking at all the bags wondering if I should arrest him now or see just how far we could take this.

Sgt. Gillespie came in the front door thinking the suspect was already in custody. He saw all the bags of weed, an uncuffed suspect and me looking back at him with one eyebrow raised and assumed rightly that this was all still in progress. I noticed him put his badge back in his pocket like I had done a few moments earlier.

"Who are you?"

The suspect inquired while looking nervously at the plain clothes Sergeant.

"That's my ride, he's cool."

I explained.

"Well… ok"

It was right about then I felt the need to kick it up just a notch.

"I need just a little over an ounce"

For legal purposes, an ounce and above is a different charge than under an ounce. This was starting to turn into a numbers game. "Sure, It will be $150.00"

I had used up all my buy money and had to borrow some cash from Sgt. Gillespie. I handed the suspect the extra cash, picked up four more bags and then had this exchange with him.

"Do you have an evidence bags I can put this in?" -me

"Evidence bags….evidence bags, I have some plastic bags!" -him.

"That will do".

The suspect scurried into the kitchen to grab us some evidence bags.

At this point I should point out that the suspect was obviously under the influence of something. Whatever he had taken appeared to have some sort of progressive effect because he was a little more unsteady on his feet then he had been when he first started helping me out.

While he was in the kitchen, two more officers came in wondering what was taking us so long. I told them he still didn't know we were police right before he walked back in.

"Who the hell are you?" The suspect inquired of the two newly arrived officers.

"I'm here to check your cable" Responded the first one.

"I'm here to help him." Responded the second one.

"Well, ok then." Came the slurred response.

"Do you have any other illegal narcotics you would sell me?"

I asked, trying to ride this hot streak as far as I could before it's inevitable collapse.

"Illegal narcotics? I've got some soma pills."

Came the somewhat suspected reply.

"That'll do."

The suspect knelt on the floor, poured some pills from an unmarked pill bottle on the floor and slowly began sliding them with his index finger from the pile to a spot one foot to the left, counting slowly.

"One, twooo, threeeee…"

Meanwhile, I'm on my knees facing him sliding some of the pills from the new spot over to the old spot also using my index finger. Just for fun.

"Quit man, you're screwing up my count."

Our dealer was crashing fast.

Suddenly a stranger walked into the house, looked around and decided everything was cool. He then ask for and was sold two quarters of weed by our mascot pot dealer. As he exited the house an undercover officer excused himself to step out and smoke a cigarette. This happened three more times. Apparently business was brisk at this particular location.

The fifth guy was a little more "Woke" as the youngsters like to say. He walked in, looked around and claimed loudly,

"I don't need anything, I was just stopping by to see how you were doing. You look like you're doing pretty good."

He then left, probably feeling a lot better about himself than when he walked in.

At this point it was starting to look like we were going to have to call it ourselves. The paperwork alone was going to take a couple of hours if we stopped now. Sgt. Gillespie decided to roll the dice one more time before calling it a day.

"Can you get us a pound?"

Gillespie asked the now rapidly fading dealer.

"Sure, just got to make a call."

The dealer replied before leaning back on the couch, closing his eyes and drifting off into a deep sleep, complete with snoring.

A couple of weak attempts were made to wake him but he never got more than four digits entered into the phone before falling back asleep.

"Hey buddy!"

Sgt. Gillespie said while tapping the sleeping subject with his badge.

"Police are here!"

The suspect awoke once more and his eyes grew wide while looking at the badge and then the circumference of the room containing more hippie looking folks also holding badges. You could almost see the tumblers in his brain slowly turning as he began to put all the pieces of this puzzle together. His response was classic.

"Who's snitching?"

Aftermath

For the record, the case was retired due to the intoxicated state of the suspect. Pretty much all we got out of it was a good story. Sometimes that's all you really need.

He Made me Whoop Myself

No Law Enforcement Officer likes to have a complaint filed against them. Regardless of the outcome of the investigation, it's still something that stays in your personnel file. When an officer gets in trouble the media will often bring up the former complaints from the personnel file without mentioning the outcome of the investigations. Many, many suspects claim they will be filing a complaint or lawsuit at their first opportunity. The vast majority fail to follow up and are more venting than anything else. It's not a very happy time for anybody.

During my period in the Crime Suppression Unit, we had to fill out several use of force forms commonly referred to as 108's because that was the number assigned to that particular form. An officer could touch a suspect without using the form but if force was required such as forcefully grabbing or physically pulling a resisting suspect, the form had to be completed.

During a hand to hand drug buy, the ratio of suspects who attempt to pull away or escape is right around 99% for obvious reasons. As far as the suspect knows, it's just he and a man who just announced he is a police officer trying to get him handcuffed. They can't help but make the attempt, I'm sure I would too. Back up officers are only a few seconds away, but the suspects would have no way of knowing that.
We filled out quite a few 108's. We also charged quite a few people with resisting. On particular night court commissioner began denying our resisting warrants by saying,

"I'm not going to let you load up charges on these guys".

That put us in a vulnerable position. We were using force against people who were not resisting as far as the courts would see it. It wasn't long before the situation worked itself out.

I had purchased a dilaudid tablet from a street dealer who had flagged me down at an intersection known for dilaudid sales. When I announced that I was an officer and grabbed his arm, he immediately complied.

"You got me."

This dude was the perfect felony arrest. If it had been captured on video it would make the perfect template for how to go to jail drama free. Neither of us had an issue with the other. Once I had him in the booking room, he was un-cuffed and left un-cuffed because we were getting along swimmingly.

We made small talk about the normal stuff dudes talk about while waiting to see the commissioner. As we walked into night court, I noticed it was a pretty good crowd. Night court was a form of free entertainment for many folks who enjoyed watching the show and on a good night it was better than the circus.

After being sworn in, I began to give my probable cause for the arrest. The arrestee suddenly and without warning began barking loudly like a dog. The courtroom fell silent except for his loud incessant barking. Next, he dropped to all fours and began crawling around the courtroom on his hands and knees barking at the top of his lungs.

"Sit!"

I commanded, as it was the first thing to pop into my head. The crowd roared.

"No! Bad! Sit! Stay!"

I yelled while grabbing the suspect by the shoulders as he was leaping to his feet. He grabbed an affidavit in his teeth that had been on the corner of the commissioner's desk and shook it violently. Pretty much exactly like a dog would.

"Get him out of here!"

The Night Court Commissioner screamed.

Another officer and I pulled him out of night court and back into the booking room where he immediately began acting normal again.

I never asked him why he had acted like that. I'm sure I meant to, but never got around to it. I was just glad I was there to see it live.

As I went back into Night Court to get my affidavits signed, the Commissioner immediately lit into me.

"Detective Whitehurst! Don't you ever bring a suspect in here acting like that un- handcuffed, do you hear me?"

"Ma'am, he didn't act that way till he saw you."

"Well, you should have got him under control quicker." She responded.

"Did you see how he kept struggling while we were trying to get him under control?" I asked, knowing her answer.

"I sure did, I was afraid he was going to get loose and come at me. He was fighting."

"Notice how we are not requesting a resisting warrant?"

"Yes?" She replied, her voice a little softer with the inflection of a question.

"It takes a little more than that for us to ask for a resisting warrant."

She never turned us down for another one again. Years later I would read an article about this incident in News of the Weird.

Suspects threaten in the funniest ways. I was transporting a man with several outstanding warrants to the booking room for processing. He had started out with the usual threats about having me fired before coming out with something a little more unique…

"I'm going to beat my face against this screen and tell the judge you beat me up!" He yelled, saliva flying. I immediately pressed record on my pocket microcassette recorder.

"I'm sorry, did you say something?"

He repeated it again just like before with the recorder picking up every single word.

Game on.

"You just go ahead and do what you feel you need to do." I said, successfully fighting back the urge to giggle.

BOOM! The suspect slammed his face into the Plexiglas screen that separates the arrestee from the arrester.

"What do you think about that?" He asked, just a hint of pride in his voice.

"I've seen better." I deadpanned feigning indifference.

BOOM! Round two as he slammed his head once again into the shield.

The suspect wasn't really causing much damage as the natural instinct to not hurt one's own head was having an effect. I let him do it about four more times by the time we pulled up into the sally port. it about four more times by the time we pulled up into the sally port. His forehead was a little red though, I'll admit that.

Once I got him out of the back seat of the patrol car, I rewound the micro cassette tape and let it play. The suspect heard his plot falling apart in his own voice.

"I'm going to beat my face against this screen and tell the judge you beat me up."

I would be lying if I told you I wasn't enjoying this. You could almost see the tumblers in the man's brain scrabbling to find a plan B as we shuffled on into night court.

"Just serving outstanding warrants Your Honor." I said as the Night Court Commissioner looked over towards the suspect.

"Your Honor, this Police man made me whip myself!"

And scene.

Dan Whitehurst

Caught a Fat Girl

After nearly four years in CSU, I knew my time was getting short and I would soon be rotated back to patrol. I really didn't want to go back to wearing the uniform and dealing with everything it entails.

I caught a break and was assigned to the Armed Robbery Unit on a temporary basis during what is known as the Robbery Season. The detectives referred to it as the Robbery Season but most people refer to as The Christmas season. With more people shopping and carrying cash, the number of robberies go up. Our job was to stake out areas and markets with a higher probability of being robbed. It's not an exact science.

I didn't catch any robbers, but I did chase down and catch two of four suspect who bailed out of a stolen car in front of me. For some reason two of the suspects fled on foot stayed together side by side. Both of them were handicapped by their sagging britches. They kept having to pull them up while running. I was able to grab both and drag them to the ground, one on top of the other. I guess I should note they were both around fifteen and smallish.

When an opening in robbery came up soon after our temporary assignment I applied for and got the job.

Nashville had one of the top rating robbery units in the nation when it came to cases cleared by arrest. These guys were good. They were also some real characters.

One of the bigger differences in working the Crime Suppression Unit and the Armed Robbery Unit was the team vs individualistic aspects of the two groups. In C.S.U., we were usually always together working on the same case. In Armed Robbery, around twelve detectives (give or take depending on whether or not we are fully staffed) investigate somewhere around 2500 reported cases a year, usually independent of each other. The detectives are split up in two shifts. Eight to Four Thirty and Four Thirty till one AM.

The detective units did not have tracking devices in their cars or tachographs. A tachograph is a small machine in the trunk of patrol cars that records speed, movement, and emergency equipment activation. It was often referred to as an "Iron Sergeant." Not having one of those or a tracking device was pretty sweet.

One day I decided to take advantage of the situation and slide out a little early from work. Who would know, right?

As I was pulling into my neighborhood I noticed the apartment complex near my house had a tiny bit of smoke creeping out from the shingles. I suspected it had just caught fire.

I pulled into a parking spot near the area where I had seen the smoke. The maintenance man was standing outside staring at the smoke.

"Called 911 yet?" I asked.

"Doing that now", he replied while running away towards the office. I started banging on doors and yelling for people to get out and get out now. The maintenance man joined me and together we attempted to evacuate the effected portion of the complex. As the smoke intensified, we started kicking the doors open of the units where nobody answered. In retrospect I'm not sure that was the right move.

The added oxygen may or may not have had an effect, but the fire seemed to kick into another gear.

Suddenly we heard screaming coming from behind the building. We both ran to the back of the building and saw two young women standing on the balcony. The stairwell was fully engulfed in flames and they had no other option than to jump.

They were both around 20 years of age. One white, one Hispanic. The white girl was pretty heavy. The Hispanic pretty thin.

The white girl decided to go first. This might be a good time to note that the maintenance man was pretty thin as well.

Together we caught the young woman and the three of us kind of collapsed into a pile. Gravity has the same effect on the big boned that oxygen has with fire. It's an accelerant.

The young woman was understandably hysterical. She hugged me and said I had saved her life and that she was going to write the chief of police and let him know what I had done and get me a medal. While she is telling me this, I'm trying to gently move her out of the way to try and make room for the second young woman who was now screaming for help and that she did not want to die.

"We've got you, now Jump" I yelled, trying to do so with authority.

"I'm scared!" She screamed back, as the fire from the stairwell started to ignite the edge of the balcony.

"Jump!" I repeated, not trying to mask the anger in my voice. She had to do this. Nobody could save her but her.

"But I'm afraid you'll drop me!" she sobbed.

"We caught your fat friend!" I screamed, totally without meaning to phrase it quite that way.

The young woman took a deep breath, closed her eyes and hurled herself over the balcony railing putting her trust in two complete strangers. We caught this one with no problem.

I directed the women to move away from the building as we went back to knocking and kicking on doors. The Fire Department arrived and immediately went to work putting water on the fire. Most of the residents had evacuated at this point.

The last one I saw exit the building was from the apartment under the stairwell that had been fully engulfed in flames. A middle aged man, he came out of the apartment looking much disheveled. He looked around as if he was trying to figure out what had happened, all the while the flames were burning above him. His right foot was charred and he appeared to be missing a couple of his smaller toes. The big toe was smoking. He was also smoking a cigarette. I didn't do any follow up, but I bet he had something to do with the fire.

For the record, the big boned white girl never wrote that letter.

Dan Whitehurst

The Mayor of Shantytown

I was once the mayor of Shantytown. The title was quite unofficial.

As an urban patrol Officer I spent quite a bit of time with the homeless. They usually put on a big show when they were arrested but more often than not they didn't get physical, especially when the temperature dropped into the teens. A roof over your head and a guaranteed release after a few hours is a small price to pay for disturbing the peace or public intoxication.

We had some pretty famous street people, famous at least at the local level. One lady had a beehive hairdo that had matted in place and was infested with some sort of bugs created a maze of tunnels throughout it. She was usually kind and grateful when officers gave her coffee or change. I heard she had been the victim of a drink spiked with hallucinogens and went from normal to homeless almost overnight. It kind of makes you think.

Preacher was one of the nicest, most respectful homeless people I ever met. When he was sober. The longest stretch I had seen him sober was maybe three days.

When he was sober he would dress up in an old suit and tie, comb his hair and sit on the bench outside of Jail Docket. Sometimes he would fall asleep and nobody ever bothered him. He died with people seated all around him on that same bench.

I was one of many people that saw him that day and assumed he was asleep. He was in the same position hours later when they wheeled a gurney in to remove his body.

Henry was another local legend. A reputed sadomasochist who always wanted to fight when he was getting arrested, even if he wanted to be arrested. I once threatened to unarrest him and pull him out of my car if he didn't calm down. It worked. The rumor was that he became sexually aroused when he was beaten so people went the extra mile to avoid fighting him.

Long after I left police work Henry's name came up in a conversation with another retired officer.

Apparently this officer had arrested Henry, who smelled worse than usual on this particular day, and he had asked Henry if he had experienced an "accident in his pants". Henry claimed he had not.

Once Henry was placed in the patrol car for transport, the question was repeated again resulting in the same negative response. He was asked a third and final time while at booking for a grand total of three denials for those keeping score.

As Henry was changing from his civilian attire into his orange jail house jump suit it became apparent that Henry did in fact have an accident and had been carrying the evidence around with him in his britches.

"Henry, I asked you three different times if you'd had an accident and you denied it every time."

Henry looked up and offered the following deadpan reply. "I thought you meant today."

The homeless are often victims of violent crime themselves. They are considered easy pickings for criminals because they often have no way of following up with prosecution even if they wanted to. When we had reports come in with homeless people being victimized it was generally because the hospital called in on their behalf as the law requires.

Sometimes they were beaten just for sport by teenagers looking for something to do, sometimes by other homeless people trying to exert their dominance. It's not a very pretty existence.

The first time I ever made my way down into "Shanty Town" was as an Armed Robbery Detective. I received a report of a homeless victim being robbed and assaulted who lived there. The address listed on the report was "The woods behind General Hospital." Usually the address for the homeless is listed as 129 7th Avenue South, the Union Mission, where they very seldom happen to be.

The report listed a suspect's nickname which indicated the victim knew who it was that robbed him. This one was actually solvable if I could just find the victim. I had plenty of cases to work, but this one became a challenge.

I was able to find the wooded area where several makeshift tents and hastily constructed sheds dotted the landscape. By a stroke of luck I was also able to locate the victim. He seemed nervous and suspicious of my intentions. Once I explained that I was investigating a report of him being robbed he actually teared up. He couldn't believe the Police Department was working for him and not against him. As he shook my hand I commented that there was a new Sheriff in town and he's also the mayor, a line I borrowed from the movie High Plains Drifter.

Before I knew it, several of the homeless from the area gathered around and listened wide eyed as my victim explained to them that the police were investigating his claim against a suspect they all knew and somewhat feared. A mama dog with about eight small puppies following her also showed up and joined the gathering. Many homeless people have incredibly strong bonds with their dogs, as the dogs do with them. I'm guessing having a dog at your side doesn't hurt the panhandling business very much either.

My next trip to shanty town was a few days later when I took a photo line up to the area to show the victim. Detective Mike Chastain came with me because he wanted to meet these folks he had been hearing about.

We stopped at the old feed store at First Avenue and Broadway and picked up a fifty-pound bag of dog food for that herd of puppies. I was glad Mike agreed to go because I needed help lugging that big bag of Old Roy down the hill.

We couldn't locate the victim during this visit but we did turn the food over to the lady with all the puppies. She thanked us both and at one point made reference to my title as Mayor. It seemed my campaign was gaining traction.

While we were interviewing the locals Detective Chastain noticed that several plastic bags had been tied to the top of sapling trees in the area around the camp. One of the residents explained that the bags were the work of one of the neighbors that was angry at his deceased mother. He continued to explain that the neighbor would defecate in the bags, pull the saplings over, attach the bag and then release them. It was all an effort to place the pooh closer to his mother. Vengeance isn't always pretty.

The next time I visited my constituents I was able to locate the victim and show him the photo line-up. He made a positive identification of the suspect and I transported him to the robbery office and night court where we obtained aggravated robbery warrants on the suspect.

Once we got back to the campsite the victim began showing his pink copy of the affidavit to some of his neighbors, proving to any remaining doubters that the justice system could work for them too. Everyone seemed pretty pumped about having this dangerous man removed from their midst and I must admit it felt pretty good to be a part of it.

While bidding everyone farewell and sharing in the enthusiasm generated by the moment, I observed a middle-aged male amputee crawl out of one of the tents. His left arm was missing at the shoulder, his right at the elbow. He struggled to his feet and made his way over to where the victim and I were standing.

The victim was enthusiastic about introducing me to the new arrival. He showed his copy of the affidavit to him and introduced me as the new mayor of Shanty town.

The new arrival was a male white, mid-forties with around a three day growth of beard and wearing oversized pants with a tightly cinched belt. It was obvious that he had some compassionate assistance with some of the day to day activities most of us take for granted.

As we made eye contact the man raised his right stump till it was pointing at me. I was about ninety percent sure he wanted to shake my hand so I went with my gut and firmly grasp his stump in my right hand and shook it as normally as possible.

The suspect was later picked up by patrol and booked on one count of aggravated robbery. I was never able to locate the victim and never saw him again. The charges were dismissed on the basis of failure to prosecute and the suspect was released back into society.

And the wheels on the bus go round and round.

What are the Odds of that?

Police tend to sweat the small stuff. They don't want your hands in your pockets while they are speaking to you, they want you to move over a lane of traffic when they have someone pulled over, they don't want everybody piling out of the car on a traffic stop. If it seems they are a little paranoid, they probably are. They earned the right to be.

Consider this odd fact. In the United States of America, one person a year is shot by a dog. Yep. In one really exceptional year, four Americans were shot by dogs. If you can imagine it, it's probably happened before to somebody somewhere at sometime and a cop probably took the report.

I read where now days police officers will touch the driver's side tail light as they approach the driver's door to leave their finger prints. They do it in order to help the investigators in case they are murdered. After reading that, I did notice officers doing that. I never did that back in my day. I did place my hand on the trunk lid and push down as I walked to the driver's door, every single time. Every officer I knew did this because every so often somebody will pop out of the trunk and shoot the officer. It's rare, but it has happened more than once, and every cop knows it.

Sometimes something very positive would happen that would leave me scratching my head and wondering what the odds of that happening were. One in a million?

In the Armed Robbery Office, pre- photo computer age, we had a system we would use to try and narrow down suspects in armed robberies. It entailed taking mug shots of every arrestee in Davidson County and categorizing them by age, height, weight, race or unusual characteristics like a missing eye or facial tattoos. When a robbery victim came in to the office, and we had absolutely zero leads in their case, we would let them look through photos.

For instance, if a person described the suspect as a male white one hundred and sixty pounds, six foot tall with light brown hair and about twenty five years of age, you would pull out a huge stack of photos from five foot ten to six foot two male whites with brown and blond hair and within a few years of the given age and hand them to them to let them look through. The detective would then sit at his desk and fill out reports and make follow up phone calls. It wasn't considered a total waste of time. Sometimes victims would pull out a photo and say,

"I don't think this is him, but he looks a little like this as far as his hair color and eye shape".

Usually we would take the photo and run them for a history, just in case, then put the photo in the case file in case someone who looks similar gets picked up. The success rate of a victim actually making a positive identification of a suspect from looking through our photo system was almost non-existent. Almost.

I had a victim make a positive identification of a suspect from a large stack of photos once. It was the top photo of the first stack I handed her, right after I set the stack in front of her. It went a little like this.

"This is him, right here on top."

"Ummm, ok, on a scale of one to one hundred, how sure are you this is the man that robbed you?"

There was no way I was going to get a warrant on this man without more than an identification from the first photo she looked at. "One hundred percent sure. This is the man, right here. I don't need to look at any other photos."

"Ok Ma'am. I'm going to see what I can find out about this guy and I'll be getting back to you."

The victim thanked me and left the office, leaving me to investigate the subject she positively identified. We had a partial print lifted by the identification section, so I took down the information on the man in the mug shot and forwarded a finger print comparison request for this subject. I almost hated to refer to him as a suspect.

The print came back as a match to the suspect. The random suspect, from the top of the photo stack. A warrant was obtained, the suspect was arrested, and he confessed the crime during the interview. One Christmas morning as I was getting off work while in the Patrol Division, I got on I-40 East and headed to my sister's house to celebrate with the family. I noticed two cars on the side of the interstate, one of which appeared to be having an issue with a tire. Two men appeared to have it under control and I so badly wanted to drive past them and get on with Christmas. It was quitting time. Then I thought about it being Christmas for them too. I grunted, turned on my patrol car's blue lights and crossed two lanes of traffic and parked behind them to see if they needed help.

While we were talking, I happened to notice all the lug nuts were off all of the wheels on one of the vehicles. It wasn't a flat tire, it was a vehicle being stripped. Both men gave up without a struggle so I can't complain, but I did miss Christmas. The early part anyway.

During the summer months I loved riding my motorcycle after I got off work. I got off at one o'clock in the morning when I first transferred to the Armed Robbery Unit. I'm sure my neighbors hated me.

One evening a few minutes after midnight, I decided to do a drive by at a particular night club that always had a lot of motorcycles in the parking lot. I was never big into going to night clubs, but I liked this one and enjoyed riding my bike to the club until word got out that I was a cop. I found out I had been outed as a cop when I walked in one night and the lead singer of the band on stage changed the lyrics to the song he was singing to,

"The heat is in the building"

That pretty much ended my involvement with the club. But this was before that.

As I was turning onto Thompson lane, the dispatcher put out a description of an armed robbery that had just occurred in Belle Meade. The suspects were described as two male blacks armed with a sawed-off shotgun. It was further reported that the suspect was beaten and forced to give his pin number and bank card and the suspect vehicle was a gray or dark colored four door.

As I was passing the SunTrust Bank teller location on Thompson lane, I noticed a male white and two male blacks all crowded around the teller machine. My initial thoughts were that there was not enough time for them to have driven to this area yet and the descriptions were off as well. I kept driving because I really wanted to check out that motorcycle scene for later. That little man in your head that tells you when you're wrong started talking to me and made me feel guilty. I also noticed how unusual it looked to see three people huddled around a teller. People generally give each other a little space at a banking machine. I made a U-turn and headed back towards the bank. I saw the subjects all get into a gold four door sedan, lowered with oversized chrome wheels.

I followed the vehicle on Murfreesboro Pike, glancing at my watch because it was almost quitting time and looking for some sort of traffic violation for a valid reason to stop them. I was driving an unmarked white Ford Taurus so they wouldn't be driving like a cop was behind them. I finally decided it was now or never, so I hit my strobe lights and pulled the vehicle over on the ramp to Briley Parkway without any violation. I didn't check out on the radio because I was certain this wasn't the suspects. No way. This would just take a second or two then we would all be on our way.

The male white driver exited the vehicle and came back to me. This is generally not a positive sign. I apologized to him for the intrusion but wanted to know if he had just used the SunTrust teller on Thompson Lane. He said he did and pulled out his SunTrust bank card to show me. This was going great, I was going to be in the wind in no time.

"Is this the card you used?"

I asked as I was handing him the card back, my job here complete.

"No sir"

He responded, making me a tad bit uncertain.

"Who's did you use?"

I asked, still thinking there was absolutely very little chance this was the suspects.

"Look sir, I don't want to get anyone in any trouble."

That's all I needed to hear. I was behind a car containing two armed robbers and a sawed-off shotgun and nobody knows where I am. All of that became very clear to me before he uttered the last syllable of the word trouble. This was about to get really serious.

"No problem, I don't want to get anybody in trouble either this close to quitting time."

I was laughing as I said it. I wanted him as relaxed as possible.

I mentioned something about the weather, then very calmly said on my walkie talkie,

"Headquarters, put me out on the Briley Parkway ramp off Murfreesboro road talking to a ten fifty-three."

I knew there was no way to ask for another car without him knowing I knew. A ten fifty-three is an armed robbery. Nobody talks to an armed robbery. I was hoping they would pick up on that and they did. I quickly turned my volume down because several officers started to speak at one time. I could hear sirens off in the distance and I remember thinking to myself,

"I love these guys"

Patrol got there, surrounded the suspect vehicle and the two remaining suspects gave up without a fight.

I think maybe at times Police Officers are not paranoid enough.

Big Jimmy Don't Like Snakes

Most people that I know have at least a degree of fear when it comes to snakes. I certainly do. I've picked them up and held them in order to prove I wasn't afraid of them, but that was just an act. I was terrified.

I even had a dog who was afraid of snakes. His name was Major. I once caught a puffer snake by putting an upside-down garbage can over him. When I would bang on the can the snake would exhale loudly which would echo inside the can. It sounded pretty neat. I called Major over and thumped on the can making the snake make his evil snake noises. Major was totally amused. He kept barking and scratching at the can until I suddenly lifted it and surprised him with its contents.

I've never seen him run so fast. As I already admitted, I don't like snakes. I took the Bible passage about snakes and man being enemies seriously. Very seriously. At the same time, I feel sorry for those rare people who have an outright terror of them. The people who would leap from an airplane if they suspected a snake was on board. The people who would sell their house if they saw a snake in the yard. I don't have it as bad as those poor souls.

I've met a few such people. Now that I'm older and wiser I do realize it is a crippling phobia and not something that should be used for my amusement. I regret most of the times I used their fear for my amusement.

Like the following example.

As a rookie Patrol Officer in West Nashville, I had both a pet store and a video rental store side by side in my zone. I would often stop in both to say hello. The owner of the pet store even let me feed his piranhas from time to time.

The pet shop had a large glass enclosure with a full-grown Boa Constrictor residing in it. He had a tree limb and a pan of water to make him feel at home. I'm guessing he was around twelve feet and ninety or so pounds.

I was curious about the snake and asked the store manager a few questions about the creature. Apparently, he took possession of the snake after it had fully matured. He also mentioned that the snake had not been socialized so he was very careful about who he would sell it to.

My normal fear of snakes does not prohibit me from looking at them or being interested in them. I can coexist in a world with snakes as long as I know where they are and what they are doing.

The owner told me a story about a man who recently came in and asked to hold the Boa. The owner warned the man that the snake had not been socialized and it would be dangerous to try and hold it. The man became indignant and claimed he had owned snakes all his life and he was interested in buying the snake but would not do so without holding it.

The shop owner relented and let the man remove the unsocialized Boa from the enclosure. That's about when the story got really interesting.

Apparently, the Boa immediately began attempting to choke the life out of the former snake expert. Both the buyer and seller were unable to loosen the snakes grasp on the man who was now in a panic. The Owner drug both the man and snake outside onto the side walk.

The cold winter air began to weaken the cold-blooded reptile and they were able to pull him off and get him back in his cage.

I found the story fascinating and was trying to tell it to the clerk at the video store next door to the pet shop.

She stopped me and told me to keep my voice down because her co worker had a phobia about snakes and would not even pick up a movie box that had a snake on the cover.

I thought she was joking. She wasn't.

"She doesn't know about that big snake next door?"

I said loud enough for the coworker to hear in what might have been my worst failed attempt at humor ever.

She quit that day.

Big Jimmy had that same fear of snakes. It didn't matter if they were gardener snakes, cobras or made of plastic. They all caused him to panic.

Someone once put a wooden snake near the door of the robbery office once and Jimmy wouldn't exit the office until it was moved. He just sat in his chair, gun in hand and stared at it.

My second worst failed attempt at humor was putting a realistic looking rubber snake in Big Jimmy's chair while we were working an extra job at the state fair. Fortunately I was able to get out the door as Big Jimmy was reaching for his pistol.

Of all the things to be concerned with as a law enforcement officer, snakes were way, way down on my personal list of things to be afraid of, but then again I have a normal fear of snakes. With Jimmy Arendall, snakes were at the top of the list at all times.

One warm summer day we loaded up and headed to an address in West Nashville to attempt to serve an armed robbery warrant on a suspect. It was Detective Arendall's case and myself, Det. Chastain and Sgt. Stromatt went to assist him.

This was around the time my arthritis was really starting to cause me problems. I had difficulty walking across uneven ground and running was totally out of the question.

When we arrived at the suspect's residence, I went to the back door in case the suspect tried to flee out the back. While I couldn't chase him, I figured I could at least grab him and make him drag me along with him to slow him down.

It's always a little nerve wracking being at the back door. You can't see what's happening up front and all you can do is listen for the knock and keep your eyes on the exit.

I braced myself as I heard the initial knock which was followed seconds later by the apparent sound of a woman's high- pitched scream. I could hear words being shouted and what strangely sounded like laughter mixed in as well. It was all I could do to focus on the exit door.

Once I heard cars being started, I assumed we were done and came around to the front to see if the suspect had been apprehended. I saw Big Jimmy backing out of the driveway, yelling out his open driver's side window,

"He can turn himself in!"

Before accelerating rapidly down the street away from the scene.

Detective Chastain filled me in on what transpired up front between gasp of air wiping tears of laughter from his eyes.

Apparently, a small snake had slithered from a small artificial pond over to the deck upon which Detective Arendall stood. Sgt. Stromatt had seen the snake but hoped Detective Arendall would not.

Detective Chastain claimed Jimmy saw the snake at the last minute and was able to get from the deck to his car without touching the ground. He also claimed that Jimmy was responsible for the screams I had mistakenly attributed to a woman.

Had I fully understood the terror felt by people with an unnatural fear of snakes I probably would have never said or done anything to put them in that state of fear.

Except for the ones targeting Big Jimmy Arendall. Those were hilarious.

The Fart Machine

I'm sure early mankind's humor was cutting edge. They didn't have the gadgets to entertain themselves like we do in the modern era. According to Wikipedia an early version of the Whoopie Cushion was used in Ancient Rome. In the 1920's, JEM Rubber out of Toronto Canada brought it back and the rest is history.

I don't know exactly when the fart machine was invented. Apparently, Wikipedia doesn't either. I do know that they started surfacing around the Armed Robbery office in the late 1990's. I consider that period the apex of flatulence humor. It was basically a remote-control triggered device that produced one of four possible flatulence sounds when you pushed the button.

Detective James Arendall was the first one to bring one into the office. It was glorious. He didn't break it out right away, instead opting to keep it secret until we all met up at the Old Country buffet for lunch.

Big Jimmy left the machine in the pocket of his vest and left his vest draped over his seat at our table while we were all headed to the buffet line. The first one back to the table was going to get it. It turned out to be Sergeant Stromatt.

Just as the good Sergeant was starting to dig into his salad, Big Jimmy started pulling the trigger. From our vantage point we couldn't actually hear the machine's retort but we could see the reaction of those walking past the table. Everyone walking by reacted in some form or another. One lady actually glared at him and said he should be ashamed of himself. He just responded meekly with,

"Excuse me."

You really don't just prank someone one time with a fart machine and let it go. It gets funnier every time. I can't explain why, it's just one of those mysteries that maybe we aren't supposed to understand. It became a normal part of the meal every time we ate there, which was about once every two weeks.

By the third trip to this buffet, Detective Mike Chastain had discovered that all the remote devices to the fart machines were interchangeable. They all activated the machines if they were in range, so he brought his own remote in to make a funny situation even more hilarious.

On two separate occasions, Chastain began hitting his remote as Big Jimmy was walking towards the exit after we all finished eating. Again, we couldn't actually hear the sounds, but we could tell when it started firing shots by the way Jimmy would pick up his pace trying to exit the building.

For whatever reason we failed to go to this particular restaurant for over two months. It seemed even longer.

Finally someone made a motion to go there for lunch again and I was almost giddy with anticipation. Again, I don't know why I find this so funny. Once we arrived, I asked Jimmy if he remembered to bring his machine. He said he couldn't bring it here anymore. When I asked him why he said he didn't know if it was the type microwaves they use or what, but something keeps setting the thing off and the last three times we came here he farted all the way out the door.

It wasn't all just fun and games. Sometimes we used the machine in social experiments to confirm what we already suspected.
By chance we discovered the remote would work even if the machine was in another room. This led to us putting it in the men's room and waiting in the hallway making small talk and stalling for time. Whenever

someone walked by the remote was triggered and a shot was fired. As best I remember, six men walked by and each one laughed or at least grinned in acknowledgement. Four women walked by and not one reacted in any way what so ever.

It wasn't really ground breaking news. I personally had always suspected that men and women had different sensibilities when it came to humor, but it was nice having the confirmation.

The Machine also made it into a court of law, in a way. I had placed the machine in the trash can of the interview room prior to Detective Arendall interviewing a suspect in a series of armed robberies.

I was in charge of recording the interview for the court purposes and was professional enough not to pull the trigger during the important parts of the interview. I was semi-professional. I waited patiently until the interview was wrapped up. As Big Jimmy placed his hands on the table and began to stand, I fired off one shot and one shot only. He got the suspect out of the interview room in record time. I never got subpoenaed to that particular case, but I like to think I brightened a couple of Jurors day.

Men and Dogs

I've never heard anyone say that they liked humans more than animals. Not once. I'm sure many people do and probably the majority would choose the human if they had to save only one. I've just never heard it expressed verbally or viewed it in print.

On the other hand, I've often heard people say they liked animals more than humans. Usually after some sort of incident that displays man's inhumanity to man starts running on a loop on the news cycle. I've always assumed it was a response based in emotion and to be honest I've probably thought it myself even if I haven't said it out loud.

I got my first dog at around age twelve. He was the family dog but he liked me best. I got my second dog a week after I bought my first house. He was all mine. He was a wolf hybrid I named Duran. Duran seemed more wolf than dog and never really acclimated to living in polite society. He jumped a five-foot fence and killed eleven pet rabbits a neighbor was raising for Easter. At twenty bucks a pop, that cost me two hundred and twenty dollars.

I had three strands of barbed wire placed on the top of my fence to try and keep him in but all it really did was make my backyard look like a concentration camp. He was very pack oriented so I adopted a Labrador to keep him company and named him Leonard.

Leonard was a rescue. His current owner was about to put him down due to his habit of chewing up wires. He had a thing for it apparently. I had Leonard for about one month. In that time period he chewed both spark plug wires off my motorcycle, chewed the thermostat wire off the central heat and air and contracted parvo.

He survived three days at the vet before passing away. Total vet bill, seven hundred dollars.

Leonard's replacement was Blazer. I didn't name him.

Blazer was a rescue as well. A full-blooded Husky who had his vocal cords removed because he lived with a breeder who felt the need to have that done. He hung his collar on the fence and choked himself to death after a month.

These dogs were breaking my heart.

I went to the animal shelter to find Duran another companion and immediately settled on an older Rottweiler missing one rear leg at the hip. I kept looking at him wondering who would adopt an old three leg dog.

Me. That's who.

During the interview to determine my ability to give the dog a good home, I was asked to describe my last three dog's lives. I told her about Duran, Leonard and Blazer. I was turned down in record time.

I left after letting the woman know that I would be buying a rottweiler with all his legs. I didn't want to tell her that, I just felt compelled to.

I picked up a copy of The Tennessean on the way home and found some Rottweiler puppies for sale in Columbia Tennessee. I purchased Jack Dempsey for three hundred dollars. Best money I ever spent.

Jack Dempsey, or Dempsey as I called him, loved to ride in a car. He also liked to sit in cars and would get in any car that had an open door and resist all efforts to remove him. It could and did get embarrassing at times.

There were times I would get tied up at work and be gone from home for over twelve hours. Somehow Dempsey was able to keep from relieving himself for unbelievable periods of time. His desire to please was one of his biggest strengths and he was a much better dog than I deserved.

Once we had a couple of suspects robbing pizza delivery drivers. They would take both the pizza and money from the driver after calling in a false order and waiting near the address. It had become so common we began wearing the pizza company's shirt and delivering the pizzas ourselves. A detective could cut a hole in the bottom of a pizza box and hold his or her gun in the bottom box while an actual pizza was in the top box. We would then deliver the pizzas ourselves and the hungry folks never knew the difference.

One day we were able to apprehend one of the suspects who was trying to rob a different delivery driver while we were in the same apartment complex. The manager gave us all the left-over pizza as a thank you.

Dempsey loved pizza. I know all dogs do, but he took it to a whole new level. I couldn't wait to get home and greet him with a warm pizza. He met me at the door looking as if he had lost his best friend. "What's wrong buddy, are you sick?"

Dempsey just stared at the floor, unable to even look me in the eye.

"I've got you some pizza!"

I held a slice out to him and he sighed heavily before turning and walking away towards the corner of the room. I followed him until he turned and sat next to a pretty impressive pile of dog poop, all the while looking like he was an emotional wreck.

I cleaned up the evidence then got on my knees and hugged him telling him it was my fault for being gone so long. He shook all over in relief, then enjoyed his pizza. He was truly a good boy.

We very well might have committed a robbery once. This was many years ago and the statute of limitations has long been expired.

I had picked Dempsey up while working the evening detail to let him ride with me for the last hour of my shift. We happened to pass a Crispy Crème with the hot light on. Stereotype or not I do enjoy a hot donut. I pulled up to the drive through window and ordered two maple glazed, one for each of us.

(Before you judge me on my dog's diet, he ate everything I ate and lived for fourteen years, four more than a Rottweiler's life expectancy.)

As the clerk attempted to hand me the bag of donuts, Dempsey totally lost his composure, climbed over my lap and stuck his head outside of the driver's side window and into the Crispy Crème window. The poor clerk turned her head away holding the bag in our general direction and screaming,

"Just take it!"

"How much do I owe you?"
I asked, while pulling Dempsey back into the vehicle from whence he sprang.

"Just GO!"

She screamed still not looking at us.

I gave Dempsey a good talking to before handing over his donut.

I said all that to say this. I understand the assumption of innocence given to animals and the lack of the same when it comes to humans.

I was assisting another detective with a homicide off of Harding Place. The victim was deceased and laying in his vehicle covered with a sheet. Months later I would be told it was a revenge killing over a set of stolen wheels.

People were doing business at the store next door. Customers walking in and out would glance over at the scene and just as quickly avert their eyes and keep walking. Some of people interviewed as possible witnesses didn't seem to want to get involved, as is often the case.

Once I had checked back into service, I pulled out onto Harding Place and started to drive back to my office to type up a supplement report. After traveling somewhere around two hundred yards I noticed what appeared to be a traffic accident in the turning lane.

I pulled up behind a car blocking the turning lane and activated my emergency lights. Two additional cars were pulled over on the side of the road and residents of the apartment complex had begun lining up at the edge of the property adjacent to Harding Place. Some were weeping.

As I came to the front of the parked car, I saw a crying woman cradling an injured dog, undoubtably hit by a car. Another woman approached with a blanket she had retrieved from her apartment.

A man who also lived in the apartment complex pulled up with his pick-up truck. The dog was carefully placed in the back of the truck and two more people climbed into the back to ride with him to the emergency Vet. My eyes may have appeared as wet as theirs.

As I was leaving, I heard several people asking around trying to find out who owned the dog. Nobody knew who owned the animal or who would be responsible for him, but they didn't let that stop them from trying to help him out.

I wish people reacted the same way to the suffering of an unknown human as they do when it's an unfamiliar animal, but as a group it hasn't always seemed like the case. On the other hand, we haven't as a group given each other much reason to trust humans.

They Never Just Quit on Their Own

One of the first things Sergeant Stomatt told me about the armed robbery business was that every suspect should be considered a serial robber when apprehended. The odds against arresting a first-time armed robber are pretty high. If you have enough probable cause to make an arrest in one case and the suspect makes an admission in that case, a detective can sometimes squeeze a couple more confessions out of them.

I've actually had multiple suspects admit and give details about every robbery I suspected them of. Afterwards I would say something along the lines of,

"Ok, I believe you, but now lets talk about this other robbery you never mentioned"

And more than one suspect responded with the following retort,

"Awe man. You know about that one too?"

While the suspect was describing those other cases, a monitoring detective would have someone looking for those cases in the case files so they could be pulled and cleared as solved. The interview room is where the iffy cases can become very strong cases. A confession alone isn't worth near as much as a confession with details he or she could not have known without actual knowledge of the crime.

There are several types of serial robbers. Usually it's a single person. If he uses a note the first time, he will probably use a note every time. Same with a mask. If he wears it the first time, he'll probably wear it every time. The do what works and if they have not been caught yet, they assume it worked. When it's groups of suspects working in unison, they hit a place a day until they get caught or something scares them or convinces them to back off. Sometimes they become more aggressive during each subsequent offense. Those are the ones that will make a detective lose sleep.

I had two cases assigned to me one a Monday that were obviously the work of the same suspect. The physical description matched and the suspect forced the female victims to undress in both cases. He also molested the victims in both cases violating them with his pistol. I interviewed the victims as best I could but I didn't have a lot to go on. I.D. was unable to lift any comparable prints, so that was out.

The next time he hit was on a couple of days later at an antique store, the female victim was made to hold her own eyelids open as he sprayed her in the eyes with pepper spray. I can't imagine the suffering she went through. He also hit a furniture store on Nolensville Road that day. He took the victim's rings off her fingers. She described one as a gold band with a pig engraved on the inner part of the ring. She described it as one of a kind which would definitely help if he pawned the ring one day. The fact that he hit two different areas in a short period of time meant he probably had a vehicle. We just didn't have any idea what that vehicle might be.

The next day we had a string of five robberies on Nolensville Road. The suspect was robbing one after another. About a quarter a mile away from one robbery, he was robbing his next one, each one further out bound on Nolensville Road. I responded to the area while the robberies were still being broadcast over the police radio. The last robbery was an attempt. The suspect entered a shoe repair shop where an armed clerk pointed a Berretta 92 nine-millimeter at him. He quit robbing for the day.

Going through the reports from the five robberies, I noticed a witness had listed a possible vehicle description as a maroon four door. It wasn't much but it was something and everybody was desperate to find this guy before he tortured someone else. Cops really do care when someone like this is running loose. They put a lot of pressure on themselves. I remember the sex abuse unit swearing off alcohol until a serial rapist was caught. He usually hit on weekends during the rain, so the unit would come in and work all the weekends that fit that weather pattern. I think everybody in the Sex Abuse Unit stayed sober for over a year.

A lot of luck always helps in these cases. Someone found a maroon Buick abandon in an apartment complex. The vehicle had been reported as stolen. In the back seat was a coke can which I.D. unit was able to process and lift one print of good quality. At this point I was doubtful, but hopeful. It was possibly the suspect vehicle, and the print was possibly the suspects, but it was a pretty weak case so far. Plus I needed a suspect to compare the print to.

The following day I got one of those gifts every detective prays for. An AFIS hit! AFIS stands for Integrated Automated Fingerprint Identification System and is a computer system in which a good clear finger print can be entered into the program and it will use it's big computer brain to rapidly compare it to every known print that had ever been entered into the system for any reason. This time they matched that print off the can to a known felon who had recently got out of prison. He also appeared to have gotten out early.

The suspect had a failure to appear warrant on him already, so we went to his listed residence to serve that warrant and see if he could be the suspect. We planned on using his new mug shot to put in a photo line-up to see if the victims could identify him.

The suspect's mother owned the residence and let us to search for him. She said she didn't know if he was home. He was. I initially started interviewing the suspect in his room. I told him we had a warrant on him, but I didn't tell him what it was for. I was also wearing my cap which was clearly marked,

"Metro Armed Robbery Unit"

The suspect was claiming that he had no right to be there and that he hadn't done anything to anyone. He was starting to get loud because he was starting to get nervous. I was looking past him and at his chest of drawers right located right behind him. I could see something that looked like a pepper spray canister partially hidden under some sort of article of clothing. As I'm staring at it, I notice a gold band next to it. As I stepped closer I could see a small pig engraved inside the band. I felt a wave of relief sweep over me. It was finally over. Well, until the next one.

The suspect was a complete idiot. He signed his Miranda waiver because he wanted to see what I knew and convince me he was innocent.

He was denying any involvement in the cases, and especially the ones where the females were raped with the pistol. I told him we had lifted his prints from inside the store but never mentioned the rapes. He admitted going in the store and talking to some women but denied anything else. I then asked him if he made them strip naked so they could not chase him when he fled. This is known as giving them an out. He jumped on it and said he did make them strip so they could not see which direction he fled. He then claimed the gun was not real. I've seen pedophiles deny and deny and deny any sexual involvement with a child till the detective asked if the child had initiated the encounter and they reverse course and make a grab for the branch they think is going to save them.

The suspect in this case admitted being inside every business I charged him with, because I told him we lifted his print in every business we knew he robbed. The victims were able to make a positive identification and he wound up getting his parole revoked and a bunch more years tacked on. He's probably out by now.

Dan Whitehurst

You Might Know My Daughter

"You might know my daughter, she was a police officer in Brentwood."

When people find out I was a police officer they sometimes ask if I know a particular officer that they know. They might follow up with a positive or negative story, depending on weather it was a relative, or maybe their arresting officer. Sometimes they just give the officer's name and ask if we've met, maybe it's a cousin that works in Atlanta or for the Alabama Highway Patrol. Invariably, I never recognized the name. The funniest one I remember hearing was from an inebriated woman who inquired about an officer she described as being a big fat slob. I told her she would have to narrow it down. I can say that. I'm kind of heavy. It was hard to keep track off all the officers on The Metropolitan Police Department. We worked different shifts and off different radio frequencies. An outside agency is a definite long shot.

I had just taped my first nationally televised comedy set on the Mike Huckabee show. The show's announcer, Keith Bilbrey of Grand Old Opry fame had just introduced me to Emy Joe Bilbrey back stage.

"You might know my daughter, she was a police officer in Brentwood." The Lady said after her husband introduced us. "She was shot in 2002. I wondered if you might know her."

I immediately remembered exactly who she was.

"Yes Ma'am"

I happened to have responded to the call, along with the rest of the Armed Robbery A Detail. We had just sat down to eat somewhere in South Nashville. I do not recall where exactly that was. I just remember the way the call came out. It wasn't an alarm. It was much more serious.

The vast majority of armed robbery alarms are false alarms. Usually accidently activated by employees or occasionally misused to report a theft or non- armed robbery related incident. I was actually in a Denny's Restaurant at Eighth Avenue North and Dominican with Officer Jerry Page when the dispatcher put out an armed robbery alarm at that particular Denny's. We were sitting across from each other in a booth and both immediately turned our radios down and started nervously glancing around the restaurant. Everything appeared to be going on in the usual way, and again, most alarms are false, but it still felt pretty creepy for a minute. It turned out it was the Denny's on Murfreesboro Road getting robbed and somehow it got changed to the one on Dominican before being put out. I think that guy got away.

Armed Robberies are dispatched on all airs, or every sector's channel generally. Before the details of the alarm are given, a loud series of annoying, but attention getting beeps are broadcast. Like a lot of officers, I would usually turn the radio down during the tones, then back up to hear what it was about. This wasn't an armed robbery alarm. This was a citizen who called into the dispatcher and reported a man walking down the sidewalk carrying a "Machine Gun" and it was walking into the Bank as she was speaking.

We jumped up and fled from wherever we were trying to eat that day and sped towards Brentwood hoping we could get there before the fight started. The fight that was no doubt coming. Nobody ever walks in and robs a bank with an AR-15 and gives up. At least none any of us have ever heard of.

We were all familiar with the North Hollywood shooting from 1997. They had been using it in in-service training for instructions on what to do and not do with such suspects. Several officers were shot. More came. That's what most officers do. Even more were shot, but in the end Justice was served. Twelve police officers and eight civilians were injured. None died despite their horrendous injuries. Both suspects were killed while wearing body armor. Over two thousand rounds were fired between the suspects and police. The officers in North Hollywood actually borrowed AR-15's from a nearby gun store in order to have a decent shot at stopping the men who were proving to be immune from the pistols of the police.

We didn't have AR's. Neither did Brentwood. This was going to be bad. We didn't quite make it there before it started. By the time we arrived, three of Brentwood's finest had been shot as well as the man who thought he could just walk in and rob a bank in Brentwood with a semi-automatic rifle.

We began interviewing the still shocked witnesses and filling out supplemental reports well into the evening hours. I interviewed a witness who had watched the exchange of gunfire by Officer Stephanie Bellis and the suspect. The man claimed he heard shooting while he was in his vehicle at the intersection. He described seeing the officer walking backwards in front of her rolling police car and exchanging gun fire with a man firing what he described as an assault rifle. He got behind his vehicle as the suspect kept advancing towards his vehicle while firing his rifle in multiple directions. He further stated the female officer came around his vehicle and told him to stay down on the ground. He said he could see she was bleeding from a wound on her arm as she continued to engage the suspect. He said he told her she had been shot, but she responded that she was fine and that he needed to stay down.

He said the last he saw was her was when she was leaving the cover of the vehicle towards the suspects last known location. When he was describing to me the way she was using her rolling car as a shield, I could hear the admiration in his voice. Later on I would see the dash cam video from Officer Bellis patrol car. It's still shown in police academies today as an example of keeping one's head and never giving up.

"Yes Ma'am. I know your daughter, She is a hero".

Sometimes I'm Not a Nice Person

One of my many faults is finding humor at others expense. Sometimes to access. My rule of thumb was that if they laughed than it wasn't wrong. If they reacted negatively, I generally felt guilty, depending on the circumstances.

This has been an issue for me since childhood. During the summers of my high school years in Camden Tennessee, I worked as a lifeguard at the city pool. It was a pretty sweet gig. We played stupid games like seeing who could wear the most ankle weights and still swim to the surface. The water in the pool started out so clear you could see the bottom. Two months later it was so cloudy you could not. I do not care to know exactly why.

I learned that while sitting still on the lifeguard stand my metabolism seemed to slow to the point where I could hold my breath for an extended amount of time. I could only do it once, then needed another break to reach those kinds of lengths again. Every couple of hours they cleared the pool for about five minutes to force a break on the kids and allow the lifeguards time to take a dip and cool off. We generally would all dive from the chair into the deep end, in spite of repeated warnings by the pool manager, Patty Primm not to do that. Apparently, she feared one of us hitting our heads on the bottom which was a distinct possibility.

One fine day, late in the summer, during the cloudy water period and during the break, I decided I would play a prank on Miss Primm. With my body totally rested and my breathing slowed, I dove from the lifeguard stand into the deep end, swam to the bottom and grabbed the drain grate and sat motionless. It seemed like an eternity, but I finally heard the splash as she dove in, fully clothed, to save me.

She laughed once she died off, but then again this was in the days before cell phones.

The second time I tried to pull the same stunt I nearly died. I was fighting every urge to surface as my lungs felt like they were on fire. I finally gave up and swam towards the surface not knowing if I had enough air to make it the required nine feet. As I broke the surface and gasp for air, I made eye contact with Ms. Primm, standing on the edge and wind-milling her arms as she attempted to abort the rescue mission. She failed and once again went in fully clothed. This time it wasn't as funny to her and I felt a little bad. I did get a half-hearted grin when I complemented her on how long she had waited that time.

That was bad, but I've done worse. Much worse. During my period with the Crime Suppression Unit I made many, many hand to hand buys of cocaine from street dealers. The first few times were terrifying as it is a well-known fact that the robbery and murder rate for people buying drugs from street dealers is pretty high. Like anything though, once you do it enough one can become comfortable if not complacent doing it.

If we took a couple of weeks off from doing the buy bust operations and focused on search warrants or prostitution, I would be nervous again when we went back to buying dope for the first couple of times. After that I went back to being too comfortable. It wasn't just me, it was all the buy officers.

Officer Kenny Dyer would sometimes stutter badly when making a buy. It served two purposes the first of which was too appear less like a police officer and the second and more important purpose was to try and make everyone listening or witnessing the deal fight to stifle a laugh. I have to admit I did admire the patience of the drug dealers.

None of them ever tried to rush him or finish his sentence for him. He would also claim the other officer was a mute which effectively kept them from stepping in and speeding things up.

Buying crack cocaine was truly like shooting fish in a barrel. Dealers would swarm the buy car and compete over who was going to make the sell, sometimes arguing violently with each other. I can understand why the residents of the neighborhoods where the dealers set up shop had such a problem with it. As the jails began to get overcrowded the laws were changed to lower the penalties for cocaine sales. The same dealers would be back on the same corners within a matter of weeks.

The solution to the lowered penalties was to make multiple buys from the same subjects then indict them. Instead of buying dope then grabbing the salesman, the new tactic was to equip the cars with hidden cameras, buy the dope and drive away. Once an officer had bought three different times from the same suspect the cases were presented to the grand jury. During this period, I made several buys from multiple subjects and only got robbed one time. It was hilarious.

On the day of the robbery, Officer Tom Rollins from East Sector's CSU was assigned to ride with me in the buy car. This was during the indictment period where we were buying and driving off while everything was being recorded for the grand jury presentation. Tom had been on several very productive search warrants and was a veteran narcotics officer. This was his first time in the buy car. I knew he had to be nervous if he was normal. As we were headed towards the project area where we would be making the buys, we had the following conversation.

Tom
"Do you ever worry about being shot when you do these?"

Me
"I've always wanted to be shot while doing one of these"

Tom
"WHAT?"

Me
"Not fatally, just shot, Not killed"

Tom
"Why?"

Me
"So when people ask me about it I can stare off into the distance and say, I don't want to talk about it"

"That's crazy"

Right about then we reached the street where the cocaine dealers congregated. As I turned onto the street I stared straight ahead and muttered just loud enough for him to hear,

"I've always wanted to have a partner shot too"

The deal went off without a hitch. The next dealer to approach us in the second area we visited wanted to see the money first. I dutifully held the twenty-dollar bill in my lap where he could see it. He made a motion as if he was reaching in his own pocket, then he quickly reached in and grabbed the twenty-dollar bill and I grabbed his wrist. We were in a stalemate.

"Bring the gun"

The suspect yelled loudly to a male subject who was standing behind him. I had a pretty good grip on his wrist, and he knew it. Normally we would have yelled that we were police and dealt with it that way, but not this time. We couldn't burn the car or ourselves as police at this point in the operation.

The second suspect reached into his jacket as if he was reaching for a gun, but never pulled it. I strongly suspected he did not have one. Both suspects and Tom all seemed to be yelling for me to let him go at the same time. He was able to break free after a few more moments and walked away. We left the area with what I hoped would be a coming indictment for aggravated robbery. By the time they had identified the suspect and put him in a photo line-up, I could no longer make a positive identification. I had bought from a whole lot of people since that day and I've never had one of those photographic memories when it comes to recalling faces or details. I always had to take really detailed notes right afterwards to keep things straight in my head.

It was an incredibly unprofessional and possibly even dangerous thing to do. He very well could have a gun. It doesn't even strike me as funny anymore. But, on the day it happened I found it hilarious. Maybe I'm learning to grow up.

Dan Whitehurst

With Apologies to Sergeant Stromatt

As I stated in a previous chapter, I got into The Crime Suppression Unit through the back door. Sgt. Stromatt, a.k.a. "Stump" didn't really have a say in it. It was by accident but never the less I understood why that could have caused some hurt feelings between us. It never did, or at least to a noticeable degree. It was a good thing too as I wound up working for him in Armed Robbery and CSU for a total of nearly 16 years.

He acquired the name Stump from his high school football days. He was built kind of low to the ground and stout. His father was a Lieutenant with the police department. I think he had kinfolk in the Dispatch as well. It was almost like he was bred to be a police officer and he was very, very good at it.

Stump began his career in the police department's radio room at eighteen years of age. At twenty-one he graduated from the academy and became a patrolman. He made the rank of sergeant relatively quick and was placed over Central Sector's newly formed Crime Suppression Unit as its first immediate supervisor.

He also had a great sense of humor and the ability to laugh at himself. It served him well because even though we all loved and respected him, we were also quite brutal in our jokes at his expense. He always laughed as hard as the rest of us when we got one over on him.

Stump had black hair, brown eyes and a slight olive type complexion. He was constantly mistaken for being Hispanic by our rapidly growing Hispanic community. Non English speaking Hispanics always tried to explain things to him. Sometimes at our urging. The look on his face when they began speaking Spanish to him never got old. It was just as entertaining the first time as the last.

The first thing I got when I was assigned to CSU was a pager. This was back in the days when everyone thought you were either a doctor or a drug dealer if you sported one on your belt. The first page I got was while I was in court on the witness stand.

Fortunately I had it set on vibrate so it didn't cause a disturbance. After being excused from the stand I went out in the hallway, found a phone and called the number. It was a pager number. I entered my pager number as my response and my pager went off again. It took three calls before I realized I was paging myself. I then understood that I needed to stay on my toes around this bunch.

We had a little game we played with Stump and the pager system. We would page him and put his home phone number in. Stump always ended his conversations with his wife with the words, "I love you," and for some reason we always found that hilarious.

We would sit patiently while he called his wife, then quietly chant, "love you, love you, love you" in unison until he said it then we would all bust out laughing. Lisa, his wife would hear us laughing loudly and ask him what was so funny. He would explain that we were messing with him, which meant he had to repeat those three words yet again. While he was giving her his explanation, we were busy chanting again because we knew he had to say it again. We once got three "I love you" quotes in one call. I think he laughed as hard as the rest of us when he was finally able to hang up.

Sgt. Stromatt worked as hard as he played. Our stats were always high and he was always involved in the takedown of the suspects or one of the first ones through the door even though he didn't have to be. It was like having a supervisor and an additional officer at the same time.

Personally, I always respected his character. He did the right thing, not the easiest thing and that's what the citizens of Nashville deserved.

Statistically, in The Armed Robbery Unit some crimes were easier to solve than others. The case of an old lady who was beaten and robbed by a stranger she has never seen is much harder to solve than when Bubba gets robbed by the guy he regularly buys dope from, but Stump wanted us working the harder case because that was the right thing to do. Statistically it might have hurt us a little but it never mattered because it was the right thing to do.

Stump had a small troll doll he kept on his desk. If was about six inches tall, had purple hair that stood up like Don King's and he wore a police uniform. It was a gift from Lisa Stromatt and he always kept it on his desk. Every night before I left the office I would pull the pants down on the troll doll and every evening when I came in, his pants would be pulled back up. Five days a week this occurred without fail. Stump would never mention it and I always assumed it was because he didn't want to give me the satisfaction.

It later evolved into me pulling his pants and shirt off, folding them and putting them beside the troll doll. Again, he never mentioned it.

On July 23rd 1997 I was in Florida with some friends. We were watching the news of the search for Andrew Cunanan, a notorious serial killer who was believed to be in the area.

I saw a post card of a group of muscular men wearing string bikinis and bought it without a second thought. I addressed the card to Detective Mike Roland in the Homicide unit and wrote the following on the back of the card,

"Having a killer time down here in Florida and wish you were here with me. I doubt you could find me though, love A.C."

Deep down I knew it wouldn't work, but I was hoping it would lead to a call to Detective Roland by the FBI. I'll admit It was a long shot.

When I got back to work a few days later I noticed that someone had placed three gay pornographic magazines in my mailbox at work. Just for the record, the mailboxes were constructed of clear plastic. I rightly suspected Detective Roland had placed the magazines in my mailbox. One has to retaliate in these type situations to maintain his or her position in the pack.

My initial thoughts were to throw the magazines away, but that little voice in the back of my head instructed me to cut out all the pictures of penises and save them for future use. There are a lot of penises in gay men's pornography. Even the advertisements have them. I wound up tossing the cut up books and was left with a legal sized envelope chock full of penises. Later that nigh before I left for home I pulled the uniform off the troll doll and taped a penis to him. It wasn't really to scale or anything and actually reached the desk by the little dolls feet. The following evening the penis was gone and the doll was in full regulation garb. Stump never mentioned it. That was his game.

For over a month I repeated this exact same procedure, so did Sgt. Stromatt. Every night the troll had a penis of various size and color and every morning he did not. I had given up on Stump ever acknowledging all my work.

About six weeks in, Stump stopped me in the hallway. It went something like this.

"Hey Dan, can I talk to you for a minute?"

"Sure Stump. What's up"

Stump looked up and down the hallway as if he was about to share some classified information.

"How many more of those penises do you have?"

"Plenty".

That was pretty much it. He didn't ask me to stop and I didn't volunteer to. It still felt like a win. I ran out of penises a few days later and that pretty much ended that little running gig.

The Armed Robbery unit had two shifts. Days and evenings. For the midnight shift one detective was assigned call out duty for each week. In order to combat unnecessary overtime, Metro came out with a rule that if a detective got called out he had to call and get approval from his supervisor which meant Sgt. Stromatt was getting calls at all hours of the night every week. He never complained or seemed irritated about getting those calls he just accepted it as part of the job. One night/early morning around two thirty am, I was called out to the scene of a robbery where a detective was needed by patrol. I washed my face and dialed up Stromatt's number. It went something like this. Stump, sounding understandably like he had just been awaken from a sound sleep.

"Hello?"

"Hey Stump, it's Dan."

"Yeah Dan, what do you have?"

"Hey man, are they still giving us those random drug test?"

"Uh….yes, I'm pretty sure, why?"

"Hey man I've got to go."

I hung up the phone, waited about thirty seconds then called him back.

"Hello?"

"Hey Stump, Dan again, I forgot to tell you they need me over on Jefferson Street for a call out. They have one in custody"

He started laughing before hanging up. I hope he got back to sleep.

Several Christmases Stump gave us all nice gifts. I once got a beautiful sweater that I really liked. I'm sure Lisa picked them all out, but it was still a really nice gift and he got them for everyone. We wrapped everything on his desk in Christmas paper. His phone, his computer, a fire extinguisher we took from another office, his troll doll. It took a whole lot of unwrapping just to find out we didn't get him anything. He thought it was hilarious.

Once I transferred from evenings to the day shift I began working directly for Sgt. Stromatt. I hated getting up early in the morning but I was wanting to have a life outside of police work.

When I worked evenings I always showed up around two hours early. I was able to make up for some of the time I spent goofing off and got to see my day shift friends before they ended their tour each day. Once I was actually assigned to days, I averaged coming in about five minutes late each day. At first it was accidental, but after Stump mentioned my tardiness I started doing it on purpose. I would time it to walk in exactly five minutes late each day. I went so far as to tell Stump I'd see him around eight thirty five the following day almost every evening. He just shook his head.

I was fortunate enough to get some awards as an investigator with the Metropolitan Police Department. Sgt. Stromatt put me in for all of them, one of them was for investigator of the year for a case I had a lot of help with.

The awards ceremony consisted of a light brunch, a certificate and a photograph shaking the Chief's hand. Stump presented me the award and totally blew me away with his comments. They were all very complimentary. Hearing him say those things was one of my proudest moments.

Freddy Dewayne Stromatt is someone I will always remember fondly. For all the things I did to mess with him he always took it like a champ. Once my career ended with the police department I fell out of contact with almost all of my police friends, Stump included. I have not seen or heard from him in years. Sometimes I can't help but think maybe he didn't really find all that stuff very funny after all.

Sorry about that.

Dan Whitehurst

With Apologies to my Mother

Police work is not as dangerous as it appears in the television dramas and thank goodness for that. I've heard a police career described as years of boredom punctuated by moments of sheer terror. That sounds about right.

My dad was a cop briefly when he was between better paying jobs. Three of my cousins, all brothers, wound up having police careers. Out of the four of us cousins only one was shot in the line of duty. Three of us were shot at unsuccessfully. It sounds like a lot of shootings till you consider that between the four of us we had close to ninety years on the job. Those shootings all combined might have equaled less than a minute which doesn't really sound that bad out of ninety plus years.

A shooting involving police is generally over with within seconds of it starting. Occasionally officers are involved in lengthy exchanges of gunfire but that is the exception to the rule. A Police Officer generally has the upper hand once the shooting starts if all other aspects of the fight is equal.

A bullet proof vest and hundreds of hours of training is going to give you an advantage in a deadly force encounter, but it doesn't ensure success.

A physical fight is a whole different kettle of fish. They seem to last forever and no matter how much training you have a larger, stronger suspect will still have a pretty good shot at overpowering a smaller, older officer. The odds of the victor finishing off the loser jumps exponentially when the suspect is the one who gains the upper hand. That knowledge alone adds an element of terror that last throughout the fight regardless of the duration.

The Patrol Division offers the greatest risk of a one on one battle. The specialized divisions tend to go in with numerical superiority and if need be, SWAT can go in with overwhelming superiority.

The majority of Patrol Officers ride alone. They try and back each other up when the situation allows it and they hope for the same consideration in return.

Unfortunately, sometimes there are no back up units available. On weekends during the warmer months there are times when every single Patrol unit in the county is tied up on a call. When an emergency arises, they put the call out and see if anyone can put their current call on hold and take the new one.

During times like this one's odds of not getting help climb dramatically. These are the times when you regret not keeping up with your running and physical fitness. I've known several officers who joined a gym or rededicated themselves to staying fit after such an encounter, usually to give it up after a few weeks until the next one.

Many people enter the police academy without ever experiencing a fist fight or violent encounter even once in their lives. Nobody left the Metro Nashville Police Academy that way. Not only did everyone know what it was like to be in a fight, everyone left knowing what it felt like to lose a fight as well.

The procedure for making sure everyone took a beating was pure genius in spite of it's simplicity. The entire class was taken to the Police Athletic League Gym which was basically a boxing gym for the department's golden gloves program. Professional fighters as well as novice boxers trained there.

Officers were paired up with no regard to size or gender. The winner stayed in the ring while the loser made room for the next fighter. You simply fought until you were beaten. Danny Jones, a former United States boxing representative who once gave Evander Holyfield a standing eight count was used as motivation to not slack off against a hurt opponent. We were told anyone who cuts anyone else slack had to fight him. Everybody went in looking for the knock out. A couple tried to turn and run but were shamed into standing and trading.

I grew up a huge fan of boxing. I have owned a heavy bag since I was fifteen. I once even trained as a boxer and had one fight in the golden gloves. It was a horribly one-sided beating that I lost, or as I like to call it finished as the runner up.

My first fight in the academy was against a friend named Andy Belew. He was smaller than me by several pounds and inches. He had also just won his fight in a close one. His nose was already bleeding and he was struggling to keep from hyperventilating from his first fight. The bell rang and he bum rushed me throwing wide punches at awkward angles. Being larger and fresher probably had more to do with it than my prior experience, but I landed some really good shots. He never gave up and kept forcing the action while I teed off on him. The fight went the distance and left me exhausted.

I took my beating in the second fight, from a guy my size named Don Davidson, then had a third fight after resting and being challenged by another friend, Bruce Bartley who had prior boxing experience. I was so mad that I had to fight again I tried unsuccessfully to kill him.

The instructors were careful to point out that there is a big difference in losing in a ring and losing on the street. In the ring nobody will take your gun and apply a coup de grace.

While firefights tend to come out of the blue, physical confrontations often come with slight clues. It usually starts with passive resistance or the phrase,

"I'm not going to jail".

Out of the many times I've heard that phrase I've never seen it work out for the suspect. They might beat the first officer but more are coming. They just need to know where to go.

I once heard a friend named Mike Lee checking out on a suspicious person. Apparently, the fight started before he was finished with his radio transmission and he was never able to give his location. At one point it sounded like he keyed up his radio long enough to say the word help.

Patrol units were flying around his zone shining their spotlights down alleyways and calling his unit number on the radio. I was terrified for him. He was located after a lady called in and said a police officer was fighting someone behind her house.

By the time we got there, Officer Lee was the exhausted victor. His uniform was filthy, and he was gasping for air. The suspect was just as exhausted as the officer, but he was wearing handcuffs when we arrived.

Most of the time a police officer fights a suspect it is not a full-on brawl. The suspect's goal is generally to get away and a large part of his effort is spent trying to escape rather than trade punches. A man who might beat you in a straight up fight is not as effective when he's mostly trying to get away from you.

I remember two fights where the outcome was in question right up until the end.

The first was a domestic violence situation I rolled up on out of the blue. A very angry man chased a hysterical woman right out into the street in front of me. I was able to mention the street name via radio before bailing out of my patrol car.

I was able to get between the two and was trying my best to calm the irate abuser. I have no idea what he was upset about, but I can't remember seeing that type anger in a man's eyes before. I was still relatively new. It seemed he was looking through me and at her. He would try to get around me to get to her and I was trying to latch onto him as he went by. I opened the rear door of my patrol car at one point as we all three ran around the patrol unit. Somehow I was able to get him between myself and the rear open door. The female was behind me screaming that he was going to kill her. As he went to make another charge for her I was able to tackle him and we both tumbled into the back seat.

This was when the suspect first began to focus on me more than her. He was trying to throw punches but he couldn't get much leverage because I was on top of him hitting him with my flashlight wherever I could make it land.

I stunned him enough that I was able to get out and close the door before he could recover. I called for back up because the suspect was not handcuffed at this time. I then tried to reassure the hysterical woman and make sure she did not disappear before her assault could be documented.

"He's breaking out!"

She screamed as I heard the unmistakable sound of him kicking at the patrol car window. I requested that the back up signal ten, which means get here as soon as possible, pulled out my flashlight opened the door and went back in.

I was able to get him cuffed after a very brutal struggle. Once he was cuffed all the fight in him was gone. He sat quietly as the back up arrived and during the trip to booking.

Domestic situations can be very scary. Emotions and adrenalin are so thick you can almost feel them in the air. Normally rational people can turn into homicidal maniacs. You'll seldom find an armed robber who has never been arrested before, but many times you can find a domestic murderer who has no criminal history.

The suspect was very cooperative for the rest of our time together. I assumed the Sheriffs department would have me transport him to General Hospital for an evaluation due to the lumps on his face and head. They actually made the suggestion, but the suspect refused and said he was fine. He then asked if he could speak to me.

I met with the suspect at the intake door. He offered his hand which I took and shook. He then offered an apology for his actions and stated that I had done everything I could to keep it from getting violent and he appreciated it.

I thanked him for his words and wished him luck in the future. He seemed like a decent sort of guy caught up in a situation he couldn't control. Just a few minutes earlier he was Michael Myers from the Halloween series.

The other fight was worse, and there were two of us verses one of them. Same neighborhood as the last fight.

A good friend of mine, Officer Jerry Page worked the zone next to mine. We frequently communicated by CB radio during the shift, mostly just trying to make each other laugh. Another favorite thing was yelling over the CB while your buddy was actually talking on the police radio. If you timed it right and he forgot to turn down his CB, you could get almost any weird comment heard over the police band.

Officer Page had me meet him at an intersection in North Nashville after saying he needed help with somebody who wasn't cooperating. The conversation went something like this.

Officer Page.
"I stopped this guy and he just walked away and went into that bar."

Me.
"You just let him walk away?"

Jerry was not the type of Officer to let a suspect walk away. He was a former wrestler and had won state titles in the sport. He was both strong and confident in his abilities.

"Well, he's kind of big and he seems to be on something."

At about that time I saw a huge and I do mean huge man come out of the bar. I hoped that was not him but deep down I suspected it was.

"That's him"

Jerry said as I began silently hoping this didn't get as ugly as I suspected it might.

We walked toward the suspect who never altered his stride as he also walked towards us. Once were within arms reach, with him continuing towards us, we began to walk backwards while facing him and trying to negotiate a peaceful solution.

"Sir, please"

"Sir please don't do this."

"Sir, please, please stop."

He wasn't stopping. He wasn't speaking. He was not open to negotiation. He was going to get in his car and drive away and nobody was going to stop him. I'm guessing he was around six foot eight and around four hundred pounds and appeared to be under the influence of something.

We had almost backed all the way up to where he had previously abandoned his car. He was getting close. Neither of us seemed to want to make the first move.

Officer Page made the first move. We went from begging to trying to overwhelm him with force in a split second. He never saw it coming. Jerry hit him once with his flashlight like he was swinging a battle axe. The flashlight bounced off him into the air and was flipping end over end shooting it's beam in several different directions like it was signaling the start of an epic event. It was.

We both jumped him and somehow got him on his stomach with each of us controlling one arm apiece. Granted Jerry was stronger than I was, but neither of us could get either arm pulled all the way behind him. He grunted one time and pulled both of us under his own massive frame in one smooth motion.

This is about when the panic started to set in. I attempted to call for help but wound up hitting him in the face with my radio instead. The battery twisted off and the radio fell silent. None of this was going the way we wanted it to go.

At some point we were contorted into a pretzel shape. I could see Jerry's radio still attached to his belt and I reached for it. That's when I noticed the suspect had grabbed Jerry's gun and was attempting to wretch it from his holster.

Jerry wore a security holster, level three. With proper training you can draw and shoot with a security holster about as fast as you can with a regular holster. The advantage to having one is that unless you know how to pull it from the holster, it is almost impossible to pull it out. Almost.

I could hear the leather tearing. The gun and holster as well were slowly being ripped from Jerry's belt. I placed my hand on my pistol before seeing the headlines flash before my eyes.

"Unarmed male black gunned down by police."

I let go of the gun and pulled my boot knife from its sheath.

"Unarmed male black stabbed by police"

I threw the knife as far from us as I could so none of us would have it. I was going to try one more time to keep from killing this man. I drew my hand across his face, found the bridge of his nose and stuck my finger into his eye socket. It seemed I could feel the curve at the back of his eye. It had no effect what so ever.

W World's Funniest Cop Compilation atcher. They knew where we were, but they had no idea what we were going through. I was able to hit the mic button on Jerry's radio and yell for help one time.

The first officer to arrive saw us all motionless on the ground. I'm sure it appeared the fight was over to observers but what they couldn't see was that we were all three straining for all we were worth resulting in us all being completely motionless. Everyone was worn out but nobody had conceded the contest yet.

"Have those other cars disregard, he's under control"

The first officer transmitted thinking this was over.

I was able to free one hand, key Jerry's radio and shout the following.

"Send every car you have."

It took several officers to get this man under control. They used two sets of handcuffs on him due to being unable to get his wrist pushed close enough together for one pair.

We transported him to General hospital where he was treated and released. The only comment he made the whole time was to inquire who hit him in the eye. The shift had ended by the time we were done. Another day another dollar.

We were working the midnight shift and I was able to make it home by seven fifteen in the morning. By seven thirty I was in bed thankful that nobody died.

At seven forty-five my phone rang. It was my mother just wanting to check in with me and see how I was doing. It was a very strange time for her to call. I told her that I was fine and everything was going well. It was then she said she had had a horrible dream and had been awake since around four AM and needed to hear my voice.

I laughed and asked what the dream was about. She said she dreamed that I had just been shot in the head. Her voice was breaking as she said it.

Before I could stop myself I blurted out,

"Wow, that's weird, a guy tried to grab Jerry's gun while we were fighting him!"

I immediately regretted those words. The next several minutes were spent explaining how rare what just happened actually was. To be honest it is rare, but not as rare as a police officer would describe it to his mother.

After we hung up, I couldn't sleep and called my mother back begging her not to worry about me doing this job. She assured me that she was ok. Within a few minutes she called me back asking me not to worry about her worrying about me.

I love you Mom and I regret every grey hair I gave you.

Made in the USA
Monee, IL
17 March 2025